The Professional Adviser's Guide to Marketing

The Professional Adviser's Guide to Marketing

Edited by
Geoff Humphrey
and
Norman Hart

MERCURY

Copyright © 1990 Geoff Humphrey and Norman Hart

All rights reserved. No part of this publication may be reproduced, stored in a retrieval system, or transmitted in any form or by any means, electronic, mechanical, photocopying, recording, or otherwise without the prior permission of the publishers.

First published in 1990
by the Mercury Books Division of
WH Allen & Co. Plc
Sekforde House, 175/9 St. John Street, London EC1V 4LL

Set in Meridien by Phoenix Photosetting, Chatham, Kent.
Printed and bound in Great Britain by
Bookcraft (Bath) Ltd.

This book is sold subject to the condition that it shall not, by way of trade or otherwise, be lent, re-sold, hired out or otherwise circulated without the publisher's prior consent in any form of binding or cover other than that in which it is published and without a similar condition including this condition being imposed upon the subsequent purchaser.

British Library Cataloguing in Publication Data
The professional adviser's guide to marketing.
1. Professional Services. Marketing
I. Humphrey, Geoff   II. Hart, Norman A. (Norman Arthur)
1930–
338.4'068'8

ISBN 1–85251–066–8

CONTENTS

Foreword: The Purpose of This Book — xi

Introduction — 1

Chapters

1 WHAT IS MARKETING?
    by Leslie Gumbrell

    Editors' Preview — 5
    A Working Definition — 5
    The Development of Marketing — 6
    Differentiation — 8
    The Marketing Mix — 9
    Marketing – a Business Philosophy — 11
    References — 12

2 WHY DO PROFESSIONAL ADVISERS NEED MARKETING?
    by Stephen Morse

    Editors' Preview — 13
    Assessing the Need — 13
    Increased Competition — 14
    The Need to Identify Customers — 15
    The Need to Segment Clients — 15
    Establishing the Nature of the 'Product' — 16
    Making the Client More Aware of Benefits — 16

The Need to Make a Profit	17
The Need for Strategic Thinking	18
What Clients Want from Professional Advisers	19
Developing a Strategic Matrix	21
Managing the Whole Portfolio of Clients	22
References	24

3 TRAINING FOR THE TASK OF MARKETING
by Norman Hart

Editors' Preview	25
The Need for Formal Marketing Education	25
Marketing Qualifications	27
Professional Marketing Education	27
Academic Marketing Education	29
Marketing Training	30
Marketing Subject Areas	33
Marketing Associations	39
Recruiting New Staff	39
Recommended Reading List	41
Marketing Organisations	42
Training Organisations	42
Marketing Publications	43

4 ANALYSING THE POTENTIAL MARKET
by Christopher West

Editors' Preview	45
Why Analyse Markets?	45
Data for Strategy Formulation	47
Research vs Sales Prospecting	51
Methods of Data Collection	53
Problems Encountered When Researching Professional Markets	59
Data Collection Services	62
The Value of Research	63
Conclusion	64
Further Reading	64

5 ANALYSING STRENGTHS AND WEAKNESSES
by Ian R. Brown

Editors' Preview	65
Making an Honest Appraisal	65
The Nature of a Professional Service Business	67
Customer Care	70
Perishability	72
Ownership	75
Intercustomer Influence	76
The Service Triangle	78
How to Gather the Information	81
References	83

6 CREATING THE BUSINESS PLAN
by Geoffrey Randall

Editors' Preview	85
Why Plan?	85
The Planning Process	86
The Planning Cycle	87
Scanning the Environment	88
Who Are We?	90
Who Do We Want to Be?	90
Where Are We and Where Do We Want to Be?	91
How Shall We Get There?	93
Detailed Planning	94
Review and Control	95
Example Business Plan	95
References	100

7 STRATEGIC MARKETING PLANNING
by Michael Brewer

Editors' Preview	101
Preparation	102
The Planning Process	102
Structure of the Strategy and Plan	103
Setting Objectives	104

	Product Definition and Sales Planning	106
	Price Setting and Sales Planning	109
	Planning for Place	111
	Planning for Promotion	112
	References	117

8 A REVIEW OF THE COMMUNICATIONS OPTIONS
by Norman Allen

Editors' Preview	119
First Principles	119
The Available Options	121
The Creative Element	124

9 SELECTING SUITABLE EXTERNAL SUPPORT SERVICES
by David Farbey

Editors' Preview	127
Preparing for Action	127
Advertising Agencies	131
Public Relations	135
Designers and Art Studios	138
Printers	138
Mailing Houses	138
Other Services	139
The Media	139
Using External Support Services	140
Some Helpful Names and Addresses	143

10 HOW TO ASSESS AND ANALYSE RESULTS
by Richard N. Skinner

Editors' Preview	145
The Need to Measure Results	145
Internal Analysis	147
External Research	155
Internal and External Measurements in Combination	157

11 MARKETING IN PRACTICE FOR CONSULTING ENGINEERS AND OTHER PROFESSIONAL ADVISERS IN THE INDUSTRIAL SECTOR

Part 1 by Stephen Morse
Part 2 by Nigel Dearsly

Editors' Preview	159
Part 1 – Industrial Marketing Techniques	159
Part 2 – How a Marketing Approach Can Be of Benefit	165
References and Further Reading	169

12 MARKETING IN PRACTICE FOR ACCOUNTANTS

by Keith Lindsay

Editors' Preview	171
Introduction	171
Importance of a Planned Approach	172
Which Markets to Consider	173
Keeping Tabs on Competitors	175
Establishing Target Markets	175
How Best to Access the Chosen Markets	177
Promotional Activities to Attract New Clients	180
The Value of Outside Assistance	184
In Conclusion	185

13 MARKETING IN PRACTICE FOR SOLICITORS

by Robert Hall

Editors' Preview	187
What Is Meant By 'Marketing for Solicitors'	187
A Changing Environment	189
The Need to Plan	190
Developing the Competitive Strategy	191
Involving the Management Team	193
What Should a Solicitor Be Marketing?	194
The Provision of Resources	195
Review Machinery	196
The Need to Market	198
Constraints	199
Conclusions	199

14 MARKETING IN PRACTICE FOR FINANCIAL SERVICES
by Kevin Gavaghan

Editors' Preview	201
Marketing Financial Services	201
The Marketing Pentagram	203
Six Pressures to Innovate	205
Significant Social Changes	208
Free Banking – an Early Recognition of Change	213
Three Case Histories	214
In Summary	224
Reference	225

Index 227

FOREWORD: THE PURPOSE OF THIS BOOK

This marketing guide for professional services is very much intended as a 'foundation course' in marketing. It is structured in such a way that it can be treated rather like a series of interactive elements.

Each of the fourteen chapters is self-contained, so the reader is invited to start at any point which may suit his or her level of awareness or perception about marketing. This book is not intended as just another academic work on the subject, but a series of practical demonstrations of how various elements of the marketing discipline can be made to work, and what the expectations of implementing a marketing programme might be.

In a professional practice, particularly in a larger practice of, say, over ten partners, it is inevitable that the attitudes to, and the expectations of, the imposition of marketing disciplines will be as varied as the numbers of intellects concerned. But *The Professional Adviser's Guide to Marketing*, it is hoped, will provide a common reference point so that all the practising partners will have similar perceptions when the subject is placed on the agenda at a partners' meeting. At least some of the prejudices might have been removed and the subject be given a slightly more positive airing.

As editors, Norman Hart and myself have selected what would appear to be a logical structure, starting with the simple question, 'What is Marketing?', and working towards the final chapters which provide extremely practical advice on the implementation of successful marketing strategies.

The previews at the start of each chapter are intended to assist busy professionals select where they wish to start, and what they wish to read. We hope that at the end of the day every chapter will have some relevance.

G. V. HUMPHREY, FCIM, FBIM

The Professional Adviser's Guide to Marketing

INTRODUCTION

If the United Kingdom is to continue to build on the foundation of recent commercial success, then it can only do so by developing and practising with ever-increasing effect the techniques and disciplines of marketing in every sector of its commercial environment. That commercial environment includes the professions.

Indeed it is the service industries and the professions which could well be the key areas of future national prosperity. Unfortunately, however, the very structure of the professional practice, 'the partnership principle', with all the democratic freedom and hazards that it brings to the boardroom table, is not very conducive to the marketing principle.

Marketing is the means of achieving the entrepreneurial ambition that usually emerges in very individualistic organisations. Such organisations tend to have very vertical structures in their early years of success, with single-minded, determined leadership. Objectives and opportunities are seen clearly and pursued sometimes with a kind of crude ruthlessness. To some this is the vision they have of 'The Marketeer'.

The principle of partnership is that of a much flatter management structure, with one end of the boardroom table just a little higher than the other – the senior partners' end of course. The problem is that while age brings wisdom it does not – alas! – always bring energy and innovative thinking. That is the gift of youth. So the entrepreneurial spirit can be much tempered by the increasing degrees of 'wisdom' as one works towards the senior end of the boardroom table.

Introduce the topic of marketing in such an environment, and opportunistic youth will perhaps see it as the way forward, whereas wisdom will perceive the risks and warn that marketing costs money. Marketing is often perceived as simply promotion, promotion equals advertising, and everyone knows that advertising is definitely expensive and anyway 'we don't believe in it'.

Marketing is *not* advertising. It is myriad things, but above all it is a fundamental discipline that should be applied to all business environments, and indeed to many other sociological environments, such as education, medicine and even the development of Christian morality.

One does not practise marketing in the way one practises law or accountancy. It is, and should be, simply the fundamental discipline of practising everything that has to do with matching resources to an environment in which those resources have a use, in a way which will produce the most effective result.

The fact is that the marketing discipline is the very core of business planning. Accountants can produce a thousand projections and spreadsheets, but if a business forecast is not based on a sound foundation, which includes a thorough understanding of the market, the service needed by that market, and the discipline or method by which that service is brought to the market, then the plethora of financial data is valueless.

In a changing world this is as true of the professional practice as for any other business. Take as an example a firm of solicitors with twenty branch offices – in effect, twenty retail outlets with a serious need for a distribution policy, to distribute skills and services in a customised way. These services need to be developed to meet customer needs, some local, some national. That suggests research, locally and nationally, with each retail unit having a disciplined input to the centre so that the management team can create the services that will develop the practice.

There has to be a conscious formulation of a presentation and selling policy, and agreed and controlled attitudes towards public relations, promotional literature, advertising, and the core corporate identity. There has to be a pricing strategy. In a word, there has to be a marketing discipline across the whole business.

It could be argued that the Chartered Institute of Marketing should be the most important, most senior, chartered institute of all. Without a sound commercial attitude all enterprise is left to struggle in a commercial vacuum.

The voice of marketing is now being heard. The realisation that you don't just apply marketing principles when you're into fast-moving consumer goods is growing.

The postwar recovery of the Japanese economy, and its incredible performance in world markets over the last 20 years, has removed all excuses for bad commercial performance. From a set of second-hand tools

Introduction

and presses for an Austin 7, the Japanese car industry now threatens to dominate the world. Was it just a fiendish dedication to hard work, a disciplined society expecting little reward for its labours, or even a ruthless exploitation by capitalist bosses?

To some degree all these reasons for success were probably present, but the key to the Japanese success was fundamental – they didn't just match their resources to the environment, they created the environment of both needs and wants. They used every marketing technique known, and at that time unknown, to match their skills to the world's market-places.

The classic example is in the home entertainment market – television, ever-evolving high standards of hi-fi, computers and their vast range of educational and entertainment opportunities – what has become known in fact as the micro-chip revolution. True, the micro-chip was an American invention, with major input from British scientists. But when it came to putting the evolving technology to commercial use, the Japanese became world-beaters. It was not just their diligence in the factory, it was their diligence in creating and developing new markets – in simple terms creating 'wants', and then being the first to satisfy those market needs, in some cases virtually on a worldwide basis simultaneously.

But let's not get carried away by the Japanese miracle. One would not expect Bloggs and Partners of East Peckham suddenly to explode into the market-place with a comprehensive legal service operating straight into the living rooms of the nation using Prestel, interesting concept though it might be. Home banking is of course already with us and soon home shopping will be. Interactive home consultancy is therefore probably technologically possible now!

The point of this example is to demonstrate that even professional services are set to change dramatically in the coming years. As those changes evolve, it will be the practices that identify the new opportunities, prepare their business plans correctly, and then market *la différence*, that will emerge as leaders of the professions in the future. Now the example is, it is admitted, intentionally a little extreme. The rest of this book is not. The intention is to provide a practical, easily absorbed and practised guide to marketing for the professional environment as it exists today.

In the professional environment the injection of marketing disciplines may at first seem strange, even an irritation. It will be likened by many to their first experience of time-logging. However, once the realisation grows that marketing is a means of enhancing reward from effort expanded, then, as with time-logging disciplines, the pain will ease.

1

WHAT IS MARKETING?
by Leslie Gumbrell

EDITORS' PREVIEW

Leslie Gumbrell, BA, DIP CAM, MCIM, is a marketing consultant and one of the faculty course directors at the Chartered Institute of Marketing. After obtaining a degree in psychology at the University of Strathclyde, Leslie worked with such well-known companies as Coca-Cola and Saatchi and Saatchi. He is also a CAM lecturer and examiner.

His chapter deals with the question 'What is Marketing?' in a simple and straightforward way. To quote, 'It behoves both writer and reader to reach a joint *practical* viewpoint of the subject as quickly as possible.'

The chapter also carries a very apt cautionary note. 'So, in addition to the previous answer to the question " What is Marketing?" can be added the knowledge that marketing is largely an imprecise tool easily open to misuse and misapplication.'

You have been warned!

A WORKING DEFINITION

Every introductory marketing text seems to start by asking the question 'What is marketing?' No doubt, and quite properly, this is done in an attempt to define the subject of the text and reach common ground between reader and writer. The question as it is asked begs an answer beginning with 'Marketing is . . .', but it rarely gets *that* response. Rather the chapter tends to explore how the term is used, or misused, by those interested enough to consider the subject of marketing at all. An exploration of marketing as an organisational, functional or philosophical science, tool, art or management skill really does little to give the newcomer to marketing confidence in the practical nature of the subject. And since the subject is being studied in the context of business development – rather than academic development – it behoves both writer and reader to reach a joint *practical* viewpoint of the subject as quickly as possible. Perhaps the consideration of where 'marketing' came from, and why it came, will help in a more rapid appreciation of what marketing is and why it is important.

Firstly, create a simple working definition of marketing, e.g:

Marketing is about bringing a product or service to a market and exchanging it for something wanted by the marketer (the person bringing the product or service).

This is loose enough to be acceptable to most marketing practitioners as a general, basic outline of what they mean by marketing. But, for the newcomer, this definition should also be recognisable as applicable to the total function of business and commerce generally. Everyone who is in gainful employment and every organisation that is selling or attempting to sell a product or service is surely adhering to this definition. Does this then mean that marketing *is* business? Largely the answer is yes; but marketing is concerned primarily with the relationships and activity of the offering organisation at its interface with the buying market.

THE DEVELOPMENT OF MARKETING

Marketing has developed as an area of study and become a management tool because, in the past, organisations have tended to ignore this interface in favour of such other factors as profit, return on capital, production efficiency, achieving maximum sales levels, optimum office staffing, work study and so forth. An example drawn from a classic 'pre-marketing' period will make this explanation clear.

Consider a blacksmith in the Middle Ages. This person would be highly skilled in the production techniques needed for trade and would probably operate a form of capitalistic monopoly within a restricted geographical area. Assume the blacksmith, as a profitable sideline, manufactures and

What is marketing?

sells iron levers. As produced by a craftsperson, these levers would be solidly made and well able to meet the purpose for which they were offered – namely to raise a cart off the ground when a wheel replacement was needed. If there existed a British Standard, or a trade association guideline, for the production of quality levers, this blacksmith would have qualified admirably. In other words the blacksmith offered an excellent . . .

- PRODUCT

Of course, in this case, what the blacksmith wanted from the buyer was sufficient money to compensate at least for labour, overheads and outlay on materials. To meet this need the blacksmith had to set a price for the product which, while relating to costs and profit margins, would be attractive to the buyer. Even though the blacksmith was a monopolistic producer, he could not set the lever price to the buyer too high, since alternatives in the form of stout poles and strong people were available. Allowing for costs and desired profit, the blacksmith had to attract the buyer to the lever option with a realistic market . . .

- PRICE

Having made the product and set the price, the blacksmith had to identify where the market was geographically, bearing in mind distribution limitations, and decide how and where this product would be sold and how buyers would expect to buy it and take delivery of it. To put it another way, the seller had to meet the buyer at the right . . .

- PLACE

Finally, the blacksmith would realise that potential buyers had to be made aware that good quality levers were available from that particular smithy. Quite probably in those unsophisticated days people would rely on word of mouth to generate product . . .

- PROMOTION

So it worked. The blacksmith had a product, an attractive price, a way to reach buyers and a method of telling them about the product. This is surely a fundamental and long-established approach that relates to every commercial and business effort. Yet marketing proponents have only fairly recently adopted these crucial elements of

- PRODUCT
- PRICE
- PLACE
- PROMOTION

and called them the 'marketing mix'! Surely this shows that marketing is only a fancy name for something that people have always done by using common sense? Not quite. Consider the blacksmith's business further. What happened when a competitor entered the market-place?

DIFFERENTIATION

The competitor did not simply look at the product being offered, the price, the place and the promotional aspects, but also considered the buyer and how the product was used and regarded by that person. Just by observation and by asking questions – conducting market research in other words – the competitor would learn that the blacksmith's customers did a number of things to the newly purchased lever:

PAINTED IT – to prevent it from rusting as it lay exposed in the back of the cart.

PROVIDED A STRAW-LINED BOX – to protect the paint on the lever.

FOUND A BOULDER – to carry in the cart for use as a fulcrum when needed.

Now, if the newly arrived competitor then made a lever that was offered already painted, delivered in a proper carrying box and accompanied by a wooden pivot or fulcrum, the lever buyers would have found *their needs* better met. Within certain limits the lever did not need to be the best in the market-place; it merely needed to be strong enough to fulfil its function –

the occasional raising up of a wooden cart! With this new approach, i.e. making a product that met customers' needs better, the competitor had an enhanced choice of pricing options over the original blacksmith. The newcomer could then have:

- Charged more for a product idea that would be *seen* as functionally better than the original blacksmith's.
- Charged the same price and stolen more of the smith's prospective sales.
- Charged a lower price and stolen virtually all the blacksmith's future market – but probably made a loss.

So, by addressing *real* market needs, as the *buyer* saw them, the competitor developed a strong selling edge over the blacksmith. This edge of course could similarly be used in other blacksmiths' territories, and the competitor could profitably see an opportunity to increase the sales territory. Now, at last, buyers in all geographical areas had an option to buy a product that better conformed to *their* ideas. The competitor had in fact enhanced opportunities in the 'place' part of the marketing mix.

Finally, with a *real selling edge to talk about*, the competitor would have become more aggressive in promotion of the product. The town-crier or local bulletin board would probably have been pressed into action.

THE MARKETING MIX

Let us review what happened in this fictional trade war. The blacksmith made a good product, at a fair price, distributed well and promoted sufficiently *as far as the blacksmith was concerned*. The competitor on the other hand identified other, extra, *buyers' needs or wants*, and by satisfying them increased pricing, distribution, sales and promotional opportunities.

If the above example is multiplied a thousandfold to reflect modern competitive situations, where organisations must continually struggle to gain customers, then one can see that the organisation that best meets customers' needs will triumph. This desire to identify and to satisfy *customer* needs, while still taking full account of the *organisation's* resources and its own needs, has given rise to a management study that has resulted in something called *marketing*.

Marketing is the management process responsible for identifying, anticipating and satisfying customer requirements profitably.

Thus the Chartered Institute of Marketing defines the concept; and the approach adopted by the lever competitor discussed previously highlights the attitude. Marketing as a management process requires that, if this process is to be followed, one adopts a customer-biased orientation towards business – an orientation that can result in real benefits for the organisation. One of the world's leading management gurus, Peter Drucker, said:

> It is the customer who determines what a business is . . . what the business thinks it produces is not of first importance – especially not to the future of the business and its success . . . What the customer thinks he is buying, what he considers value is decisive – it determines what a business is, what it produces and whether it will prosper.[1]

Clearly then marketing is something that encompasses the whole business and everyone in it. It really does mean that *everyone* in the organisation, at all levels, must believe in that oft-quoted phrase – 'the customer is king'.

In reality, while marketing is a total business attitude, or philosophy, it is also exercised as a function by practitioners. Those responsible for carrying out the marketing management process – *essentially within a market-orientated organisation* – concentrate on managing the whole, or part, of the organisation's marketing mix, namely the four Ps,

PRODUCT

PRICE

PLACE

PROMOTION

in an effort to gain the mix that will attract a number of profitable buyers to the organisation's product or service. Thus, to those responsible for marketing in a professional services environment, marketing is an activity that will involve them in analysis and actions covering, for example:

1 PRODUCT   Since most solicitors offer conveyancing services, why do some attract more clients than others? Other, cheaper, conveyancing

options are now available in the market-place. How does the solicitor compete and what product edge is offered to the buyer? Is it possible for the solicitor to enhance the service offered in order to meet clients' needs more fully, e.g. in house-exchange, where, time often being of the essence, perhaps solicitors with a reputation for rapid contract exchanges would have the edge.

2 PRICE   Obviously this is relevant to the service offered, but how then can large 'city' accountants sometimes charge more for an audit than smaller, rural practices and still get the business? No doubt the big accountants will have their views! But it is apparent that the clients will have *their* perceptions also and, since it is the clients who will ultimately specify and pay the supplier, then these are paramount. The 'accountant marketer' must know what determines perceived value in the market-place.

3 PLACE/DISTRIBUTION   How many offices, or service points, does the architect specialising in the design of private residences need? Or, put another way, how close does the architect have to be to potential clients? Are the normal '9–5' opening hours sufficient, or do customers want an after-hours service? Would easier access to the architect's services via such items as modems, hotlines, faxes, etc. attract more clients, more often?

4 PROMOTION   The dentist has professional restrictions imposed on the methods of promotion available. How can clients be stimulated to tell other potential clients about the new, unique operating procedure being implemented by the practice? What budget should be allocated to promoting the practice and how can the dentist be sure that this budget is not wasted?

MARKETING – A BUSINESS PHILOSOPHY

It may by now be obvious that 'marketing' encounters a wide range of imprecise variables as customer attitudes alter, economic situations change, competition varies, technology advances and legislation alters. No one can deny that this is the case. As Philip Kotler avowed: 'Marketing remains a difficult area of analysis and decision making.

Marketing problems do not exhibit the neat quantitative properties of many other problems...'[2]

So, in addition to the previous answers to the question 'What is Marketing'? can be added the knowledge that marketing is largely an imprecise tool easily open to misuse and misapplication. This misuse can occur whether marketing is viewed as a business philosophy, an attitude of mind, a management function or even as the descriptive term for a department. The aspiring practitioner, or user of marketing, who opts to use marketing in the wrong way, e.g. to stimulate short-term demand for bad or poor services or narrowly to consider the marketing department responsible only for advertising and promotion, courts disaster and will almost certainly see the marketing effort fail in the long term.

In conclusion – 'What is Marketing?' It is a business philosophy that sees as of prime importance the creation of customers by meeting customers' needs. It is also a management process that controls a mix of organisation variables – product, price, place and promotion – in such a way that this philosophy is actioned to the ultimate benefit of the 'marketing' organisation; and finally it is part of a description applied to those who carry out the marketing process. Something that is inescapable for the business that truly wishes to create customers for the future is best summed up by Peter Drucker again: 'Because its purpose is to create a customer, the business enterprise has two – and only these two – basic functions: marketing and innovation. Marketing and innovation produce results; all the rest are "costs".'[3]

REFERENCES

1 Drucker, Peter *Management: Tasks, Responsibilities, Practices* (Heinemann, 1974)

2 Kotler, Philip *Marketing Management* (Prentice-Hall, 1980)

3 Drucker, *op. cit.*

2

WHY DO PROFESSIONAL ADVISERS NEED MARKETING?

by Stephen Morse

EDITORS' PREVIEW

Stephen Morse has been a prolific writer on the subject of marketing for over 20 years in both the English and Dutch languages. His professional career has taken him on assignments throughout Europe, Africa, India and the Gulf States.

In Chapter 2, Stephen examines the changing business environment that is making it necessary for the professional practice to embrace the principles of marketing more actively than has been necessary hitherto. He perceives marketing as 'the essential medicine or tonic or vitamin which will provide professional advisers with larger, healthier, happier and more prosperous lives'.

It's a nice concept!

ASSESSING THE NEED

Theodore Levitt says:

> No business can function effectively without a clear view of how to get customers, what its prospective customers want and need and what options competitors give them, and without explicit strategies and programs focussed on what goes on in the market place...[1]

Before going further with descriptions of marketing strategy and marketing operations it is worthwhile to pause and ask perhaps why professional advisers need marketing. After all they seem to have done very well for themselves in the past without it (or at least without consciously embracing it, which is not quite the same thing). What has happened to make 'marketing' the essential medicine or tonic or vitamin which will provide professional advisers with larger, healthier, happier and more prosperous lives?

There seem to be six major reasons which apply to all professions. Some may be more pressing than others; some may apply more to one profession than another.

INCREASED COMPETITION

The first is that there has been an increase in competition, both real and recognised, in many professions. This has come about through two kinds of pressure. The first kind has come from 'consumerists' who seek to reduce the power of monopolies and oligopolies by introducing 'competition', so that price to the consumer may be reduced; and the second from politicians who see 'freedom from petty restrictions' as a vote-winning slogan when applied to professions that for a long time seem to have enshrined their power in anti-competitive practices such as controlled entry, fixed fees, closed shops and the like.

These pressures have led many professions to recognise that they must either embrace competition and understand how it operates or they will be forced to accept regulations aimed at creating or stimulating competition in their profession. Solicitors and estate agents are already experiencing competition from banks and building societies. Management consultants are either competing or joining forces with accountants. Architects, chartered surveyors and consulting engineers are finding refuge within design-and-build contractors from the chill winds of competition 'outside'. Dentists and opticians may advertise. Doctors next? Since it is unlikely that competitive pressure will decline, it becomes essential for professional advisers to develop what Professor Doyle calls a 'Differential Advantage' (or a 'unique selling proposition') — something that distinguishes one firm from another in the mind of a client. The commonest DA is of course a brand name, but it can also be a speciality or specialism in a particular type of advice, a total package, a geographical expertise, a special type of service – anything that can distinguish the company (practice) from its competitors. Perhaps the freedoms promised after 1992 will create or stimulate new forms of specialisation, though national cultures and attitudes change but slowly.

THE NEED TO IDENTIFY CUSTOMERS

Most professional advisers are tempted to assume that the market for their services is obvious and homogeneous. Thus lawyers serve a market requiring legal advice, estate agents those who need to buy or sell houses, consulting engineers those who need the services of a consulting engineer. The difficulties arise when these 'obvious' markets tend not to choose 'obvious' advisers, deciding either to 'do-it-themselves' or to buy advice along with some other aspect of their needs.

This sort of change has forced many professionals to reassess their market and to identify real requirements more accurately. More accurate and thus more profitable specialisation follows from a clearer picture of market needs; and this clearer picture can only be drawn by undertaking more market research, a detailed description of which appears later in this book. As those who embraced marketing early discovered, an essential starting point is knowledge of customers – who they are and what they want. Further on come aspects of how to approach them, what attitudes they have and how they may be persuaded to use the professional adviser's service.

THE NEED TO SEGMENT CLIENTS

Recent developments in customer segmentation in product-based companies have demonstrated the overwhelming importance of aiming marketing and sales efforts at a clearly defined target or set of targets. For professional advisers there is a need to segment their market in two ways, by 'characteristics' and by 'motivations' – creating a matrix with 'characteristics' (such as location or income level or age group) along the horizontal axis and 'motivations' for using the service (such as cost, reputation, convenience, range of services, etc.) on the vertical axis. Where the two aspects meet will give the professional adviser an indication of where to look for clients and what to say to them.

ESTABLISHING THE NATURE OF THE 'PRODUCT'

The realisation that the professional adviser's 'product' is 'what the client thinks it is', as opposed to what it actually is, is often the starting point for planning marketing. The adviser may have a wide range of specialist knowledge, or a very deep and specific expertise. It is the client's judgement and the client's requirement which delineate what he or she demands from the adviser. An architect's 'product' can be artistic designs and drawings, providing a 'machine for living' or ensuring that the building is satisfactory and finished on time. One can think equally of the varying views of the 'product' of lawyers, accountants, consultants and others. Clarity of definition allows better planning of the skills required to 'create' the 'product' (to operate the service) and of the physical aspects of 'production', such as offices, appropriately able and trained staff, communication systems and the like. It also allows a clearer view of the areas of market need and where the adviser can more fruitfully attempt to acquire clients.

MAKING THE CLIENT MORE AWARE OF BENEFITS

There is still an assumption on the part of many professional advisers that the need for their service is self-evident, and that therefore they neither need to be influenced by the marketing idea nor have to 'go out and sell' their advice and help. From the point of view of the client there is a much greater need today for the adviser to explain what *his* or *her* speciality can do for the client, so that both the need for and the choice of professional adviser is facilitated. Even in large organisations providing professional services — accounting practices, consulting engineers, management consultants — there is a strange reluctance to explain to potential clients the benefits they will receive by using the services offered. Many potential clients, it must be said, are also reluctant to ask 'Why should I use your services?', and this too can lead to dissatisfaction from a mismatch. Like many other aspects of marketing, identifying benefits to the client requires clear and unbiased thinking.

THE NEED TO MAKE A PROFIT

Since the basic constraints on (and of course opportunities for) any company which offers products or services to customers/clients are 'customer requirements' and 'profit' (see the Chartered Institute of Marketing's definition of marketing), then it follows that the need to make a profit is a powerful driving force pushing professional service providers into a serious consideration of the other parts of the definition; *'identifying, anticipating and satisfying* customer requirements'. So an overriding consideration throughout the processes described above must be the search for profitable opportunities, and the rejection of those activities and market needs where no possibility of profit in the foreseeable future is to be seen.

'Identifying' therefore means looking for those client requirements which will either present an increasing/expanding market or one in which the adviser can offer a commanding (premium) advantage. (See below as to where such markets may be sought.) 'Anticipating' means developing greater productivity in the provision of existing services, or new packages which can provide overwhelming advantage to clients (e.g. design-and-build or house purchase packages, including legal, survey and mortgage services in one parcel) and where the saving of overheads can in itself increase profitability. 'Satisfying' means much more than 'standing ready'; it requires positive action to discover precisely the satisfaction needed by the client, and to carry through the advice or action on behalf of the client as far as necessary.

One of the features of professional advisers' markets is the dominance in most of the influence and importance of existing clients. They influence or are personally responsible for a majority of the activity and revenue. This makes the satisfaction of clients a priority in the marketing activity.

THE NEED FOR STRATEGIC THINKING

Marketing, however, does not only have to do with the operational interface with clients. It also should (and does) have influence in the company's strategic thinking. Currently the strategies of professional advisers, which should be directed towards addressing the way clients make decisions and taking full account of their resources, can be roughly divided into three:

- 'Sitting and waiting', that is putting up a brass plate and hoping that the clients will appear. There are signs that the current increase in advertising merely adds some polish to a slightly larger brass plate. It is not clear who is the target of the advertising, nor what the advertiser would like his client to do. In some cases block advertisements merely list the names and addresses of advisers – duplicating the 'yellow pages'. Typical advertisements read: 'A name you should know in Bigtown', 'Lawyers to the Enterprising', 'Your Partners in Business', 'A good commercial law firm does more than help you clear the hurdles'.

- 'Giving good service'. This view is expressed by the attitude 'If we do a good job, clients will hear about us and bring us their problems'. Unfortunately neither the clients for whom the 'good job' is done, nor any of their acquaintance are aware that this is something the professional adviser wants talked about. This illustrates what has been called 'the better mousetrap fallacy' – the idea that someone who produces a better mousetrap will be sought out by crowds of clients. In most product companies this fallacy has been relegated to the 'old-fashioned ideas' drawer.

- 'Hustling'. This method comprises lots of PR, lots of sponsorship ('the latest thing'), lots of glossy brochures, and a marketing effort of considerable dimensions that is not aimed at the most likely or the most potentially profitable client. The waste incurred does not bear thinking about.

In recent years one of the major aids to strategic thinking has been the 'Product Portfolio Analysis', which provides a way of balancing cash now against cash in the future. Following Bateson and Moriarty,[2] there is a need for an approach to strategy which recognises the way in which potential clients buy professional advice. It must begin with the

Why do professional advisers need marketing?

acceptance of the idea that marketing calls for 'intervening in models of consumer behaviour', and that professional advisers need to assemble a model of the way in which their clients can normally be expected to behave in the process of trying to solve a problem, whether the problem has to do with insurance, banking, house purchase, engineering design or management. Figure 2.1 shows a stylised approach to this problem-solving process, which starts with the assumption that potential clients are concerned to 'reduce uncertainty' and go through a process aimed at that result. It also shows that there is a need for a period of 'assimilation' even after 'implementation' before the uncertainty is reduced. The need for the professional adviser to employ both the philosophy and the instruments of marketing is evident from the fact that the client is capable of performing most, if not all, of the stages. (One of the major competitors to professional advisers is the willingness/desire of the client to 'do-it-himself'.)

A further complication is the fact that the decision to call in outside assistance can increase uncertainty for the client. For example, at which stage should outside assistance be brought in? Should the professional adviser help in problem definition, or is that always the client's job? Which tasks should the outsider be expected to undertake? Can the adviser be guaranteed to deliver?

More complications arise for the client in deciding how many advisers should be asked to quote. (Should professional advisers really be treated like building contractors?) Most clients would prefer to start with a clearly defined problem which would lead to a competitive bid (or tender) situation. Most professional advisers would prefer to enter the process at the 'problem formulation' stage and, as it were, help to write the 'specification', for this enables the adviser to demonstrate his 'differential advantage' (see above, p. 14 and Theodore Levitt[3]) and therefore is likely to be the most profitable approach to the client.

WHAT CLIENTS WANT FROM PROFESSIONAL ADVISERS

If the client's first stage is 'problem formulation', then he requires from the professional adviser that degree of expertise which he himself does not possess. In Bateson's words: 'It is the expertise that the client pays for. It is

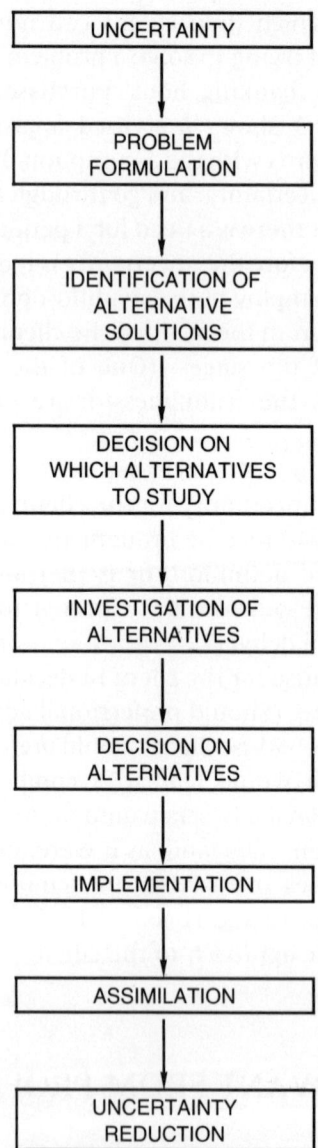

FIGURE 2.1 The client's problem-solving process (after Gummerson[4] and Bateson and Moriarty[5]).

the expertise of the firm, as embodied in its members, that represents the distinctive competence of the firm and its reason for existence.'[6] The need to recognise this is at the heart of the professional service firm's need for 'marketing', and in particular points the way to profit.

But there are going to be areas where the professional adviser has little or no expertise, though able to offer highly developed and educated intellects (a source much used by the British Government during World War II to solve problems varying from decoding ciphers to the original development of operational research), and this can do duty as the other end of a conceptual spectrum stretching from 'expertise' to 'brains'. 'Expertise' implies that we have done exactly the same job before, and therefore implies skill in diagnosis, recommended courses of action and implementation. 'Brains' implies that we are bright, intelligent and trained people, who probably learn faster than your people, even though we have not done anything like this before.

If one creates a spectrum like this, then the profitable end is 'expertise', where premium prices can be charged; the 'brains' end can be seen as a 'commodity' where competition can keep the pricing very low. (An illustration of the latter is the proliferation of companies in the computer field offering 'bodyshop' possibilities, programmers and systems analysts who are hawked around to cover the more boring implementation tasks at minimum hourly rates.) Additionally it is very difficult to persuade clients that your 'brains' are better than those of any other firm, and it is difficult to charge clients for *your* 'learning time'.

DEVELOPING A STRATEGIC MATRIX

To enable a relationship to be developed between the client's decision-making process and what the professional adviser can offer, it is worthwhile to create what might be called the Bateson matrix, which can show the strategies that might be pursued with a single client and an indication of the dangers of an unbalanced portfolio of projects. It thus demonstrates again why professional advisers need to consider marketing both in philosophical and pragmatic terms.

As can be seen from Figure 2.2, the 'Expertise'–'Brains' Axis derives from an assessment of the strengths and weaknesses of the firm in relation to the markets approached. The vertical axis condenses the client's problem-solving, as shown in Figure 2.1.

	'Expertise'		'Brains'
Problem formulation	A		D
Identifying alternatives			
Assessing alternatives			
Implementation	C		B

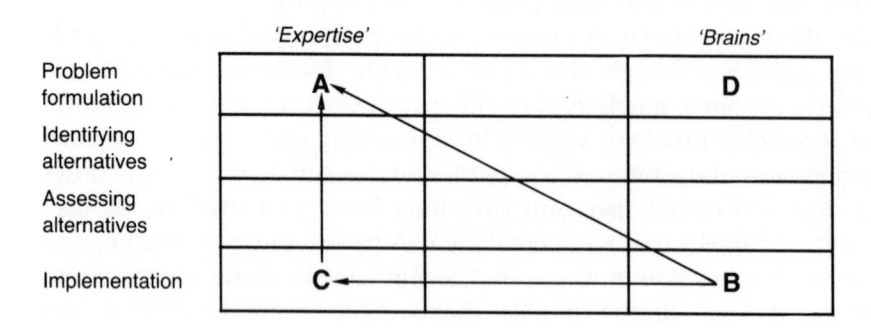

FIGURE 2.2 Bateson matrix

Using the matrix first to describe the relationship between the firm and a single client, take as an example a company specialising in software engineering which employs a number of programmers. Approach to a new client will always meet the resistance of uncertainty as to (a) whether there *is* a problem and (b) whether the software firm has the appropriate expertise to solve it. It is therefore most likely that, by approaching their potential client in Area B – 'Brains'/Implementation – the firm will be able to compete, perhaps at an unprofitable hourly rate, and be taken on. From then on the firm's task is to try to gain expertise in the company's business to two ends – more 'implementation' work (towards Area C) and 'problem formulation' work (Area A) which may not yet have arisen. The success of this strategy will depend on the ability of the implementers to identify possible areas where the firm can apply its expertise and to pass them back to the company (B to A).

MANAGING THE WHOLE PORTFOLIO OF CLIENTS

The manager in a management consultancy, the senior partner in an architectural practice, and the senior consultant of an engineering consultancy are all faced with existing constraints – a fixed amount of employee time, a fairly inflexible range of expertise, and an existing client base and the need to make a profit, both now and in the future. At this stage the matrix can help to position projects both current and potential. Careful analysis of existing projects should be made to decide what kind of advice is being offered to clients.

If there are projects in Area A where expertise is being used to help clients formulate their problems (architects, consulting engineers, estate agents should find their projects in this area), then these should be generating profits *now*. The firm would expect to have a strongly visible 'differential advantage' and would set its charges (hourly rates, day rates, block fees, percentage commissions) accordingly.

The projects in Area B are partly investments for the future and partly short-term cover for overheads, and could be distinguished by the direction of the arrows out of the area towards either A or C. They are unlikely to be profit-producing now. Strategic activity should be aimed at trying either to use the expertise gained to move up to Area A, working for the same client, or seeking other clients with similar profiles, where the newly gained expertise can be put to profitable use.

Developing expertise in implementation will, almost by definition, be a very difficult product to market profitably (look at the number of hand-to-mouth typing and secretarial services). If the firm finds that it has many projects/assignments in Area C, careful thought needs to be given as to their potential for development upwards to more profitable areas.

Both the small 'high-flying' practice and the large well-established firm of professional advisers can probably afford to have projects in Area D, where just brains and intelligence are being offered to identify and assess the client's problem. The 'high-flyers' can take the risk, because that's what makes them 'high-flyers'; the large well-established firm may well be tempted by a belief in its own image (think of some large American management consultants) to take on very risky problems in the hope of reaping rich rewards. Mistakes can be costly. Professional advisers entering Area D should perhaps be well covered by professional liability insurance!

In conclusion, using the Bateson matrix can demonstrate the need for marketing input into strategic thinking. Additionally it can indicate not only aspects of pricing strategy to cope with both competition and the major aspects of clients' requirements, but also promotion and sales strategies to cope with strategic needs, and the level and directions of after-sales service.

REFERENCES

1. Levitt, T. *The Marketing Imagination* (Free Press, 1983)
2. Bateson, J.E.G., and Moriarty, R.T. 'The Service Project Portfolio', unpublished article, 1980
3. Levitt, *op. cit.*, Chapter 4
4. Gummerson, Evert 'Producer Services Marketing with Special Reference to Consultancy Services', Working Paper at Workshop on Marketing of Services, Aix-en-Provence, 1977
5. Bateson and Moriarty, *op. cit.*
6. Bateson and Moriarty, *op. cit.*

3

TRAINING FOR THE TASK OF MARKETING

by Norman Hart

EDITORS' PREVIEW

Norman Hart, MSc, FCAM, FIPR, FCIM, is managing director of Interact International Limited and a faculty course director of the Chartered Institute of Marketing, College of Marketing. He was for 13 years the director of the CAM Foundation, and is author of a number of textbooks that are recommended reading for students of marketing. He is a visiting fellow of Bradford University Management Centre, and in 1986 became the first professor of Public Relations in the UK.

While Norman readily admits that 'Career success in marketing and selling depends, and always has done, on three factors – personal qualities, knowledge and luck', it has to be stressed that without the *knowledge*, personal qualities and luck are not given their best chance of success.

The chapter covers all the aspects of marketing training and modestly only includes three of Norman's own books in the recommended further reading list.

THE NEED FOR FORMAL MARKETING EDUCATION

This chapter considers what knowledge is required by a marketing practitioner, and the various ways of achieving it. Consideration is given to marketing education, which breaks down into 'academic' (mostly full-time) and professional (mostly part-time). Following this, a review of marketing training takes in short courses and seminars together with opportunities for in-company programmes. Finally, some mention is made of other sources of marketing knowledge, such as meetings and memberships, books and periodicals.

Marketing education takes many forms and for long in the UK its principal manifestation has been in short courses and seminars. It still is, for that matter, and in terms of short-term expediency there is every reason why these should continue to flourish. But marketing these days is far too serious a management function to be left to gifted amateurs who have had a few days' informal training from time to time. The need now is for properly structured comprehensive courses of study leading to either academic or professional qualifications.

The stumbling block has not been that you cannot teach marketing and selling, but rather you should not bother to. This particularly reactionary stance is based upon the proposition that either you have the right personality to sell or you do not, and nothing any evening class or university attempts to do will affect that particular home truth. The point that has been missed and continues to be missed is that, given the right amount of drive, enthusiasm, creativity, persuasiveness and hard work, there is still an important further dimension, namely knowledge, which is necessary for success. Knowledge never has been offered as an alternative to personal qualities, but simply as an important addition, the more so now that the whole business has become more sophisticated.

Career success in marketing and selling depends, and always has done, on three factors – personal qualities, knowledge and luck.

Which are the right personal qualities depends on which particular branch of marketing a person happens to be in, since they clearly differ as between a salesman, a manager, a researcher and a copywriter. But the fact of the matter is that they are a combination of inherited and acquired characteristics which even the best of educators can do little about. True, they can be encouraged and developed – self-confidence is a case in point – but they mostly cannot be taught.

Now luck might seem to be too simple a part of the formula for success to be credible, and perhaps 'judgement' ought to be the word. But what is judgement other than a combination of experience (knowledge), good sense (personal quality) and luck. Being at the right place at the right time has had an awful lot to do with successful marketing achievements.

So that leaves knowledge, and whilst in large part this will be knowledge gained the hard way by bitter experience, there is a growing body of expertise which is documented and which is teachable. While the other two factors are independent variables and you cannot do much about them, knowledge is something anyone can set about gaining deliberately and as a positive effort to improve the chances of a successful career. The very fact that a person does take such a course of action in itself speaks volumes for his or her motivation.

Since people are a principal asset of any organisation, it follows that any improvement in the performance of individuals must add to a collective improvement not just in operating efficiency but also in giving a company an additional competitive edge. In addition, if it can do that for a company, then on a broader scale it must add up to an improved performance at a national level. It will not come as news that what we lack as a nation is the ability to exploit our innovations. What may not have been expressed before, however, is that the solution to the problem lies at least in part with sales and marketing education.

MARKETING QUALIFICATIONS

Marketing and, to a lesser extent, selling, are taught and often examined at an introductory level in a very wide range of courses. Largely one thinks of courses laid down by the Royal Society of Arts and by the London Chamber of Commerce and Industry. But a number of basic business courses – National Certificates and Diplomas – include marketing in their syllabuses, and secretarial courses increasingly touch upon it as well as upon completely diverse subject areas such as home economics, banking, engineering, design, distribution and so on.

PROFESSIONAL MARKETING EDUCATION

The Chartered Institute of Marketing pioneered professional or vocational education first in sales management and now in marketing. Its courses are taught all over the world and its standards are high and rising. The teaching base rests largely with evening classes at colleges of further education and polytechnics, but it is backed by other alternatives, such as correspondence courses. For most students a course of study leading to the Institute's Diploma covers a period of 3 years' part-time study, and Table 3.1 indicates the range of subjects in which a student is required to demonstrate competence.

TABLE 3.1 Range of subjects covered in the Diploma of the Chartered Institute of Marketing

Year	Subjects
1	Fundamentals of marketing
1	Economics
1	Business organisation
1	Elements of statistics
2	Practice of marketing management
2	English business law
2	Behavioural aspects of marketing
2	Financial and management accounting
3	International aspects of marketing
3	Marketing management – planning and control
3	Marketing management – analysis and decision
3	Marketing communications

Hard on the heels of the Chartered Institute of Marketing comes the CAM Foundation, which operates as an educational and examining body for no less than twenty-three associations and institutes. Its expertise lies clearly in the marketing communications field, and its origination came out of a combination of the well-established examinations of the Advertising Association, the Institute of Practitioners in Advertising and the Institute of Public Relations.

The modular structure of the CAM syllabus is such that the complete range of marketing subjects is on offer and, as with the Institute, the main base of studies is in local colleges and polytechnics, as well as correspond-

Training for the task of marketing

ence courses. CAM does, however, operate its own guided studies, as well as a number of specialised tutorials and intensive courses for graduates.

The CAM scheme is open to people over the age of 18 having five GCEs, two of which must be at 'A' level. Table 3.2 gives the outline of the curriculum.

TABLE 3.2 The CAM scheme curriculum

	Certificate
1	Marketing
2	Advertising
3	Public relations
4	Media
5	Research and behavioural studies
6	Sales promotion and direct marketing

	Diploma
1	Management and strategy (CORE SUBJECT)
2	Consumer advertising
3	International advertising
4	Business to business advertising
5	PR management
6	PR practice
7	Sales promotion management
8	Sales promotion practice

Note: Passes in three subjects are required to qualify for the CAM Diploma.

ACADEMIC MARKETING EDUCATION

There has been, and still is, a good deal of debate about whether marketing alone is a proper subject to be taught at undergraduate level. In practice there is only one bachelor's degree in marketing, and that is at Strathclyde University. The fact of the matter is, however, that there are many business studies first degrees which have a large marketing component, and indeed it is unlikely that any of the business/management-oriented qualifications would allow a student to graduate without at some stage covering the marketing function.

At a more advanced level, marketing is part of a number of masters' programmes, including most MBAs, and is also covered in higher diplomas, particularly the DMS. While such qualifications are unashamedly academic with a quite deliberate intellectual content, they stretch into the real world of business partly by virtue of the growing professionalism of the teaching, and often by having a substantial period of the courses on industrial attachment to offer a practical insight into business operations. Figure 3.1 covers the gamut of marketing qualifications.

MARKETING TRAINING

The distinction here between education and training is that the former leads to a qualification whereas the latter does not.

Training activities fall into two initial categories, namely external and internal, both of which have advantages and disadvantages. These will be considered before going on to a detailed breakdown of fifteen subject areas which in some respects are considered necessary for the complete operation of the marketing function.

In-company training

What skills are required by existing staff over and above what they already have in order that the organisation can be said to be operating within a marketing framework? The application of what is known as 'gap analysis' will identify exactly what is required. Start then with a list of what is wanted, maybe taken from job specifications, then list all those attributes which the various members of staff already have, and the difference clearly indicates the subjects and the numbers of people requiring them.

For instance, one subject heading will obviously be 'an understanding of the marketing concept'. It may be that in addition to the people actually

Training for the task of marketing

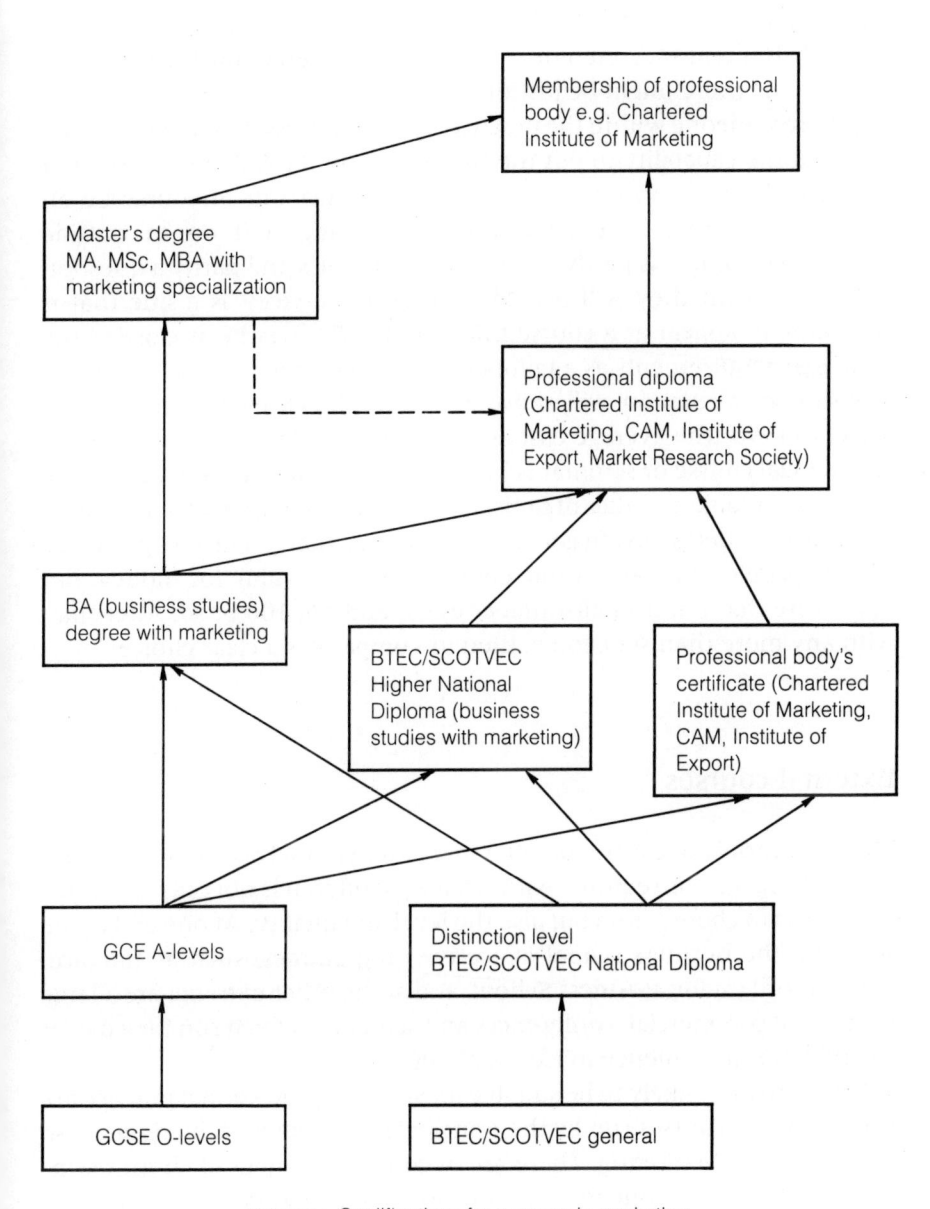

FIGURE 3.1 Qualifications for a career in marketing

engaged in marketing, perhaps just one or two, there is also a need for a high proportion of staff to have at least an understanding of what it is all about. This might mean ten or twelve people, whereas for the subject of 'advertising' there might be just one.

Is there someone within the practice with the necessary knowledge, the time and the capability to put the subject across? Probably not. So it is a matter of bringing in outside consultants, which can of course be an expensive business. The alternative to sending staff on to outside commercial courses is partly a matter of economics and partly a question of how relevant they will be. 'Marketing for services' is a title that is beginning to appear as a course title, but it will never be as close to the particular requirements as a tailor-made programme.

A simple calculation will show where the break-even point lies. At present (1990) the average cost per day (non-residential) for an outside commercial course or seminar is just under £200, and the average cost of using a reputable training organisation for an in-company training programme is £1,000 a day. In general it can be said that if there are just three or four people, then an outside course is the best value for money, but make sure that it is a small-number event and not 100 or so. After that, with any more than six people, then in-company is a clear choice.

External courses

The wide variety of courses on offer makes it extremely difficult to be sure of matching what is required with what is on offer. It is not only the range of subjects to choose from but also the level and quality. At one end of the scale are the business school executive programmes, such as Harvard, INSEAD or London Business School, and at the other extreme are a large number of commercial 'conferences and seminars' which run for a day or so and have an audience in excess of 100.

What are most likely to be suitable for staff in a professional practice are the one-week courses run by the principal management schools and also the College of Marketing. There are of course a number of shorter seminars, and as long as one looks to the more reliable trainers, these are less expensive. There is some doubt, however, as to the value of just one day unless the subject is highly specialised.

While the disadvantage of using an outside course is that it will not bear directly on the specific needs of the organisation, it does have the benefit of bringing together delegates from a wide range of different businesses, and their interchange of problems and solutions proves in practice to be very valuable. Furthermore, as long as delegate numbers are low, say ten to twenty, any seminar leader worth his salt will quickly adapt to the needs of the delegates, covering their specific interests.

A list of training establishments is given at the end of this chapter.

MARKETING SUBJECT AREAS

There is a very wide range of subject areas which need to be addressed to cover the whole marketing spectrum. For convenience these have been broken down into three groups – specialised functions, personal skills, and management. Some people will feel the need to take in the whole range, while others will think it best to concentrate on just a few.

- Specialised functions
    Advertising
    Sales promotion
    Market research
    Public relations
    Direct mail
    Telemarketing
    Selling

- Personal skills
    Writing (letters, leaflets, editorial, house magazines)
    Speaking (personal presentations, negotiating)

- Management
    Strategic marketing
    Planning and budgeting
    Product development
    Pricing and profit
    Sales management
    Consumer behaviour

Since there is considerable confusion, even among marketing professionals, as to the meaning of such terms as listed above, it may be useful to enumerate just what is meant to be covered by each term.

1   Advertising

This is commonly taken as referring to paid-for time or space in all the 'above the line' media, which is jargon for those media which pay a commission to advertising agencies. These include newspapers (national, regional and local), television, radio, magazines, cinema and posters. In discussing the use of such media, consideration would also be given to the role of advertising agencies, the advertising plan, budget, briefing, creativity, copy testing and campaign evaluation.

2   Sales promotion

It is argued by some that more is spent on sales promotion than on advertising. It all depends on the functions covered by the term. The biggest budget item relates to premium offers on fast-moving consumer goods (FMCG). But it also takes in all point-of-sale incentives as well as free samples, branded goods, competitions, business gifts and the like. Within the term 'below-the-line' (i.e. media which do not offer an agency commission) can also be included exhibitions, direct mail, sales literature, and sometimes even sponsorship and PR. In industrial marketing, 'sales promotion' is sometimes used to refer to all activities to do with the promotion of sales, including advertising and other above-the-line media. In other words, it takes the broad meaning of 'promotion' as in the four Ps of the marketing mix.

3   Market research

Here it is necessary to learn of the existence and purpose of all the main research techniques so as to be able to understand the jargon and the reasoning of the market research specialist. Purists will contend that there is a different meaning to 'marketing research', but here the two terms are taken to be synonymous. Thus one must look at the use of research to measure market size, location, competition, product perception, company image, buying motivation, advertisement copy testing, media coverage, and campaign evaluation. Any course of study should also cover the selection of a consultancy, briefing, interpreting results and assessing a budget; also the limitations of any particular research technique.

4 Public relations

Commonly this is taken to relate to the use of editorial publicity by use of 'press relations'. Any course of study, however, should embrace the very much broader function of building and maintaining good relations, and thus a good reputation, between an organisation and its various publics. Press relations have an important part to play, with press releases, press receptions and press visits. But there will be many other activities to study, including all the media which can contribute to good employee relations, for example, and then financial audiences, local community, government, and many special interest groups.

5 Direct mail

In the first instance consideration should be given to sending a letter, an object, or a communication through the post to a potential audience. This calls for the building of mailing lists (nowadays data bases), creating some form of compelling message, and then the whole mechanics of printing, stuffing, posting, responding and analysing the results.

It is convenient to study also under this head a relatively new function known as 'direct marketing', but more properly 'direct response marketing'. This is where an offer is made of a service (or product) with a view to a customer placing an order direct as opposed to going through the intermediary of a retail outlet or a salesman. The offer can of course be made by a press advertisement, though direct mail is used more often, and increasingly the telephone.

6 Telemarketing

Simply this is the use of a telephone in the marketing operation. Consideration should be given to the role of the telephone in market research, in answering enquiries and also to following up, say, a direct mail shot or in cold canvassing.

7 Selling

Though the idea of selling seems perhaps not quite suitable for professional services, the fact is that all such service organisations are engaged to a greater or lesser extent in selling. It must of course be carefully suited to the business, in which a brash 'hard sell' would certainly be counter-productive. But the selling process needs to be studied, starting with customer requirements, then on to making contact, to personal selling, negotiation, countering objections, clinching the deal, and so on.

8 Writing

Writing is one of those skills that can be improved by practice, and hence there is a big opportunity for training here. Courses usually devote time to writing in a number of specific styles and then subjecting the results to criticism. Over and above what is good or correct English, the phraseology, structure and length of a written piece will vary according to whether it is to fit into a letter, leaflet, press release, poster, film or prestige brochure. What, in many established professions, has become accepted as the norm over the years must periodically be examined to ensure that the writing style fits the customer's frame of reference as opposed to the company's Maybe the question 'What impression am I trying to create?' should be asked, coupled with the question 'What impression do I actually create?'

9 Speaking

As with writing, just about everyone can benefit from training in speaking. No matter how talented or poor a person is, a great deal of improvement can be achieved if only from having a presentation recorded and then played back. But more than this, the preparation, the prompting, the visual aids, can all be learned, and even the pace of delivery, the pauses, the avoidance of verbal clichés, and so on. Training in speaking needs to cover personal presentations, negotiations and perhaps speeches and media interviews.

10 Strategic marketing

For those involved in the management of professional services, day-to-day marketing must be set aside from time to time in order to address strategic issues connected with the overall and long-term business development. Issues which must be considered include 'What kind of business do we wish to become?', 'How do we set about it?', 'What should our reputation be?', 'Do we have the resources?' Such issues need to be learned by top management.

11 Planning and budgeting

Once corporate objectives have been set, and a strategy to achieve them laid down, the need now is to produce a marketing plan, based upon the marketing mix, and then to cost it. The plan will encompass research, 'product' development, distribution, pricing, advertising, PR, selling, sales promotion, service and profit contribution. Such a plan can only be produced by a marketing professional, since a great deal of judgement is required in the absence of any firmly identifiable facts. Similar expertise is required in formulating a budget, the basis of which is the 'task method', which centres around the tasks to be achieved and a considered estimate of the cost of all the activities needed to achieve them.

12 Product development

This is a formal management discipline which has to be learned. For 'product' of course read 'service'. A study must be made of product life cycles, product profitability, the product mix or portfolio, the cost of launching new products and the likely failure rate. Products must be seen to be transitory, subject to change in demand to keep pace with fashion, culture change, legislation, affluence and technology.

13 Pricing and profit

Management in professional services must look at pricing from a new perspective, as being based not on what it costs but rather on what the market is prepared to pay. The service might have to be cut back, or expanded, or changed, but eventually people will pay what they perceive to be a worthwhile price and nothing more. A change in profit perspective might also be required. The view must be that a given and targeted profit is the basis of all planning and subsequent endeavours rather than simply the difference between whatever income the business has managed to generate and the costs incurred in generating it.

14   Sales management

Management training in general is required, and in particular marketing management. Sales management, however, has been highlighted here as it must seem to some a most unlikely activity for a professional practice. Who, for instance, could imagine having a sales manager of an accountancy practice? But not to have a person performing this function is to miss a trick. What are the sales forecasts and targets for each of the products? How will sales leads be obtained and followed up? What are the sales territories and who should service them? What is the conversion rate of enquiries to quotations, to orders, to repeat business? What incentives are there for the sales staff? All these questions add together to make up the function of sales management.

15   Consumer behaviour

This is perhaps a somewhat academic subject for a professional practice, and for some it will seem remote, but it is in reality the fundamental basis of all marketing. What in fact motivates a person to choose you instead of your competitor? Why, in the first place, employ an accountant at all, or a solicitor, or an architect? Plenty of people do without them. Then if the decision by a person is to go along the route of professional advice, what are the factors which causes one supplier to be chosen as against another? Is it price, is it reputation, the personality of a partner, a third-party recommendation, impressive premises, or what? The issue is worth studying, since only with a good understanding can marketing resources be invested in activities which will give the best return.

MARKETING ASSOCIATIONS

One of the options open to people specialising in marketing within a professional practice is to take time out to meet those who specialise in marketing and related functions in other organisations. The obvious first thought here is to look to membership of the local chamber of commerce, and this can be valuable, especially as some of them put on a number of useful and inexpensive seminars. A number of institutions and associations have marketing programmes and qualifications, and in addition provide a regular series of meetings, local and national, which offer a useful opportunity for an interchange of knowledge and viewpoints. The Chartered Institute of Marketing is the most important body to consider, for it provides just about every service that one could wish for. Then there are a number of specialised bodies that might have a particular appeal, for instance, the Institute of Public Relations. Names and addresses of such organisations are given at the end of this chapter.

RECRUITING NEW STAFF

One of the options when developing marketing in a professional practice is obviously to recruit existing marketing executives from the mainstream world of commerce and industry. This is a straightforward procedure of matching qualifications against job specification, and perhaps using a specialist marketing recruitment consultancy to advise on selection.

At some stage in the growth of marketing operations, a complete newcomer is going to be required and in this instance there is a relatively new source, namely the business studies graduate. For many, there is still the rather strange British preference for an arts graduate from a respectable university, but this is in the process of change, and it is as well to know what is on offer both at first and second degree level.

So what makes a business studies degree? The first thing to forget is the suggestion that they are constructed by theoretical academics and taught by failed businessmen. The structure of courses varies widely across the many institutes that offer them, but they are put together by combined teams of businessmen and teachers, and faculties comprise highly qualified practical people who have held responsible and successful positions in industry.

A typical example of the subjects covered over a 3-year period is the course at Bradford University, outlined below. Starting from basic core subjects, students are encouraged to specialise in those areas which particularly interest them. For example:

Year 1: Finance; statistics; computing; economics; law and psychology.

Year 2: Marketing; production; choice from financial management, management science, applied economics, psychology and work, managing organisations.

Year 3: Choice of five out of seventeen subjects, including advanced accounting, planning and control systems, international business, personnel management, business policy, production management, strategic marketing, market research, industrial relations.

Such degree courses are available at some thirty-five universities and thirty polytechnics. Courses at the latter are validated by the CNAA. A further dimension of many of the polytechnic courses is that, in the second or third year, substantial periods of industrial placement are arranged to give a practical input to the subjects being studied. For this reason, most CNAA degrees cover a 4-year period, with one year set aside for work experience.

The degree of Master of Business Administration (MBA) is still regarded by many as an American invention, with a variable reputation, but it has produced an over-demand from organisations within British industry and commerce. Typical students will have taken a good honours degree and spent some time in relevant employment before being accepted on one of these courses, which are run mainly at the various business schools dotted around the country. They usually require a further 1 or 2 years of full-time study, though there is a growing number of part-time opportunities.

To quote from the Bradford Management Centre:

Two features characterise the MBA programme. First, a comprehensive and integrated sequence of courses aimed at providing the fundamental knowledge and skills of management which are basic to any high-level career. Second, the opportunity to specialise in a particular field of interest. The aim is to ensure that the MBA graduate can not only make a significant contribution on entering management, but also have the background and capacity for career-long self-learning.

Variety of subjects

The subjects on offer at Bradford are extremely varied, embracing core subjects and a choice of options, followed by a wide range of further choices. Core subjects and initial options include management science, economics, finance, production and marketing management, organisational behaviour plus international business, corporate planning, business policy, industrial relations, and general management. The additional choices include management accounting, consumer behaviour, industrial marketing management, managing product innovation, legal aspects of business, collective bargaining, advertising, marketing strategy, and multinational corporations in the world economy.

RECOMMENDED READING LIST

Marketing
Crouch, S.   *Marketing Research* (Heinemann)

Davidson, J. Hugh   *Offensive Marketing* (Gower Publishing Company)

Delozier, M. Wayne   *The Marketing Communications Process* (McGraw-Hill)

Hart N. A. and Stapleton, J.   *Glossary of Marketing Terms*   (Heinemann)

Kotler, P.   *Marketing Management* (Prentice-Hall)

Wilmshurst, J.   *The Fundamentals & Practice of Marketing* (Heinemann/IM)

Advertising
Director's Guide   *Choosing & Using an Advertising Agency* (The Director Publications Ltd)

Farbey, A. D.   *The Business of Advertising* (Associated Business Press)

Hart, N. A.   *Practical Advertising and Publicity* (McGraw-Hill)

Public relations
Bernstein, D.   *Company Image & Reality* (Holt, Rinehart & Winston)

Hart, N. A.   *Effective Corporate Relations* (McGraw-Hill)

Haywood, R.   *All about PR* (McGraw-Hill)

Howard, W.   *The Practice of Public Relations* (Heinemann/IM)

MARKETING ORGANISATIONS

AA (The Advertising Association)
Abford House, 15 Wilton Road, London SW1V 1NJ. Tel: 01 828 2771

Chartered Institute of Marketing
Moor Hall, Cookham, Maidenhead, Berks SL6 9QH. Tel: 062 85 24922

IPR (Institute of Public Relations)
Gate House, 1–3 St John's Square, London EC1M 4DH. Tel: 01 235 5151

ISBA (Incorporated Society of British Advertisers)
44 Hertford Street, London W1Y 8AE. Tel: 01 499 7502

Market Research Society
175 Oxford Street, London W1R 1TA. Tel: 01 439 2585

Marketing Society
Stanton House, 206 Worple Road, London SW20 8PN. Tel: 01 879 3464

TRAINING ORGANISATIONS

Ashridge Management College
Berkhamsted, Herts HP4 1NS. Tel: 044 284 3491

BIM (British Institute of Management)
Management House, Cottingham Road, Corby, Northants NN17 1TT. Tel: 0536 204222

CAM Foundation
Abford House, 15 Wilton Road, London SW1V 1NJ. Tel: 01 828 7506

College of Marketing
Moor Hall, Cookham, Maidenhead, Berks SL6 9QH. Tel: 062 85 24922

Cranfield School of Management
Cranfield, Beds MK3 0AL. Tel: 0234 751122

Henley Management College
Greenlands, Henley-on-Thames, Oxon RG9 3AU. Tel: 0491 571454

Interact International Limited
10A High Street, Tunbridge Wells, Kent TN1 1UX. Tel: 0892 515222

London Business School
Sussex Place, Regent's Park, London NW1 4SA. Tel: 01 262 5050

Marketing Improvements Limited
17 Ulster Terrace, Outer Circle, Regent's Park, London NW1 4PJ. Tel: 01: 487 5811

MARKETING PUBLICATIONS

Campaign
   22 Lancaster Gate, London W2 3LP. Tel: 01 943 5000

Industrial Marketing Digest
   7–11 St John's Hill, London SW11 1TE. Tel: 01 228 3344

Marketing
   22 Lancaster Gate, London W2 3LP. Tel: 01 943 5000

Marketing Week
   St Giles House, 49–50 Poland Street, London W1R 5LH. Tel: 01 494 0300

PR Week
   22 Lancaster Gate, London W2 3LP. Tel: 01 943 5000

Sales & Marketing Management
   Georgian House, 31 Upper George Street, Luton, Beds LU1 2RD.
   Tel: 0582 456767

4

ANALYSING THE POTENTIAL MARKET
by Christopher West

EDITORS' PREVIEW

Christopher West, BSc (Economics), is a graduate of the London School of Economics, and is managing director of Business Marketing Services Limited. He is a lecturer, author and broadcaster on management and marketing matters, and has personally carried out a number of European-wide industry studies.

This chapter gets down to the serious business of analysing the potential market, the first essential step in the development of any serious business plan.

Christopher West not only examines the need for greater knowledge but demonstrates the most practical ways of acquiring that knowledge. There is also a timely warning of 'paralysis by analysis', i.e. of attempting to acquire too much information to eliminate all business risk. 'The acquisition of information does not guarantee success. It helps to make correct decisions, but it does not replace the creative spark that is essential for all good marketing.'

WHY ANALYSE MARKETS?

In the professions success can be measured in at least two ways. The first is based on the quality of the service provided and the resultant esteem that accrues from peers and clients. The second relates to the financial return to the partner, partners, shareholders or stakeholders. Client satisfaction is a valuable asset but does not, on its own, pay the bills; nor does it guarantee full employment. Like all businesses, the professions have become increasingly competitive and, distasteful though it may be, individual practitioners have to promote themselves increasingly in order to win and retain clients.

Traditionally the professional has relied on the quality of the service provided and his reputation in order to keep existing clients and ensure a succession of new clients. A reputation for excellence disseminated by word-of-mouth recommendation, and supported by a web of referrals from one professional to another, has been the keystone of the marketing effort. The professional has therefore been inclined to equate his ability to diagnose a problem and prescribe a solution with his ability to attract and hold clients.

Unfortunately, the two are not the same and skill at the profession is no longer enough to guarantee a succession of clients. Competition between an increasing number of professionals, all equally skilled in solving clients' problems, has changed the nature of professional business just as it has other service and manufacturing businesses. The professional has been forced to become proactive in the search for clients; those who wait for the clients to find them do so with increasing disappointment. Identifying the client, reaching him *at his time of need*, understanding his requirements and convincing him that *you* are best suited to solve his problem have assumed priority over simply being a well-known, excellent practitioner. This in turn has created an increasing need for formalised marketing and market-planning programmes in professional practices, which have replaced the intuitive actions that have been successful enough in the past.

In all businesses the need for marketing and planning expands as competitive pressures, risk and the direct and indirect penalties of failure increase. The requirement also grows as managements move away from territory with which they are thoroughly familiar into new businesses. It also grows as businesses increase in size. While it may be acceptable for the lone practitioner simply to react to the demands placed on him, the large and diversifying practice with numerous staff to keep busy cannot afford this luxury. For such practices a formalised marketing programme, in which sales and profit objectives are set out together with service level, segmentation, pricing and promotional strategies by which the objectives will be met, is essential for survival.

Market planning and market research walk hand in hand. In order to plan a marketing programme practices must have access to accurate information. Experience, judgement, intuition and trial and error are important inputs to the process of determining what should be done, but in rapidly changing and competitive markets the planner needs the added guidance of an information base if he is to avoid wasting time and misusing resources. What commander in the field would plan a campaign without access to a map of the terrain, estimates of the enemy's order of battle and intelligence showing the disposition of the enemy's resources and his strategic objectives? Business planners have similar needs. Indeed, their requirements can be more acute than those of military commanders. In battle the objectives, in terms of the ultimate goal and the ground to be gained, are usually reasonably clear and the terrain over which the action will be fought is generally visible. In business the market-place is rarely understood to the same extent, and as a result it is often difficult to set realistic objectives let alone define the best means of achieving them.

Market research uses a number of proven techniques to provide planners with information about the markets they hope to service. It can cover a wide variety of topics for an almost equal variety of marketing applications.

DATA FOR STRATEGY FORMULATION

In the words of Theodore Levitt, 'If you don't know where you are going, any road will take you there.' The marketing strategy for a business, be it a professional practice or any other type, must set out clear objectives which are supported by a statement of how the objectives are to be met. A plan for the development of a professional practice of any size should show, at least:

- the sales levels or fee income that can be achieved within the market being serviced
- the future growth in sales that can be achieved
- the types of customers to which the service should be sold
- the unit prices that can be charged
- the resources required to service current and future sales and the resultant cost levels that will be incurred
- the profits that will be made.

For a more advanced strategy the programme can be extended to include:

- the 'package' of services that should be offered in order to maximise the appeal of the supplier to clients
- the level of market share at which the market can be controlled
- the extent to which price premiums can be charged and the conditions which need to be met for this to be feasible
- the extent to which 'branding' will enable objectives to be met
- the image which should be projected to clients
- the promotional techniques that have the greatest impact on clients
- the promotional messages that clients are most susceptible to
- the vulnerabilities of competitors.

These considerations may seem overtly commercial to those preoccupied with the skills of their professions. However, in an age in which businesses have to be run as businesses, rather than for the sole benefit of the clients or as vehicles for the gratification of the staff, they are as relevant to the professional as to the supplier of detergents.

Market research provides a response to market-planning issues by seeking information which will assist the planner to make decisions. Sales targets must bear some relation to the volume of demand either in the market as a whole or within the specific segments from which an individual practice is seeking to draw its revenues; customer targeting implies that customers have been identified, together with their requirements; image development programmes require knowledge of criteria by which clients evaluate suppliers and the characteristics of suppliers that they find attractive.

Market research is commonly associated with the study of customers, but, although this is in large measure true, there are a number of other topics which can provide a valuable input into a marketing strategy, particularly the study of competitors and the factors that will create a competitive advantage. The normal concept of marketing relies on a customer-based strategy in which customer needs are identified and the supplier sets out to meet them at a price which will yield an acceptable profit. Increasingly, strategists feel the need to support the customer-based strategy by a programme which provides suppliers with a clearly differentiated profile in the market, an image and a service package which is superior to those proffered by competitors.

The information which will permit planners to define a workable marketing strategy generally falls within the following topics. The precise requirements will vary from profession to profession and from practice to practice.

Quantitative market information

- the current level of demand for the service in the country as a whole and/or in the regions being serviced by the practice
- the customer base for the service and the relative importance or uptake of each customer group
- the range of complementary services purchased by the client base
- competitive suppliers of the service and the share of market held by each
- past trends in demand for the service
- projected trends in demand for the service

Customer analysis

- the identity of the decision-maker for the service and the level and type of interaction with others within the purchasing unit
- the criteria by which clients assess the ability of professionals to meet their needs
- the performance of suppliers on each of the key customer evaluation criteria
- the current image of suppliers among clients
- the extent to which clients feel the need for changes to the service and the types of changes that are required

- the means by which clients identify potential suppliers of a service and the relative importance of each
- the range of prices paid for the service
- client reaction to prices
- exposure of clients to promotional media.

Competitor analysis

- analysis of competitors' strengths
- analysis of competitors' weaknesses
- the means by which competitors seek to attract clients
- the methods by which competitors defend their market positions
- financial and other resources available to competitors
- the marketing activities of competitors
- relationship between competitors and their customers
- financial performance of competitors.

An information base should be specified in a form which will enable the professional practice to break away from precedent and generate a measure of uniqueness which will clearly differentiate it from competitors. In essence this comes from knowing who the customers are and their precise requirements, knowing how clients feel about individual professionals and the foundation of their preferences and prejudices, and recognising any gaps that exist in the current range of services that is available or in the way in which services are offered. Marketing is often associated with new developments and change, but change for change's sake is rarely profitable and there is normally much to be gained from a better appreciation of the current business. In markets as traditional as those for professional services, advantage can be created as much from doing common things uncommonly well as from doing the uncommon.

RESEARCH VS SALES PROSPECTING

Because many professional practices are small, they have a justifiable preference for dedicating their limited financial resources to activities which will bring a rapid return. Their principal concern is to win customers rather than engage in seemingly academic exercises. Market research, which does not provide a list of customers, can easily be perceived as academic. In fact customer targeting is relatively straightforward and, carried out in isolation, does little to help the practice increase its market penetration, revenues and profits. The difficult task is ensuring that the practice concentrates on those customer groups that will bring the highest returns, and then defining marketing programmes which convert them from potential customers to actual customers at fee levels which yield a better return to the practice. To do this requires a depth of understanding which is immeasurably greater than customer identification.

Before embarking on a research-based marketing route, careful consideration must be given to the benefits that will accrue. Research, like all marketing tools, will increase operating costs and must be justified by a corresponding or greater benefit. It is easy for the professional marketer to decry the traditional methods of gaining clients and to show how practices must become marketing-orientated in order to survive. It is equally easy for practices to appreciate the advantages that can be gained from a better understanding of their client base. Unfortunately, the translation of those advantages into better operating performance is far from easy and there is a real danger that practices will increase costs but not revenues. The researcher has little to contribute to this dilemma, other than by performing his function sufficiently well to ensure that profitable strategies can be defined on the back of his research findings, by assisting in the preparation of the strategies and by pointing out that data has a value *only if it is used.*

Paralysis by analysis

If sales prospecting is too limited, there is an equal danger in attempting to acquire too much information about markets. Practices which seek to eliminate all risk from their business decision-taking by acquiring ever-increasing volumes of market data will be sadly disappointed. The acquisition of information does not guarantee success. It helps one to make correct decisions but it does not replace the creative spark that is essential for all good marketing. It has been often said that marketing is an art, not a science. Those who attempt to reduce it to a set of scientific principles become moribund.

It must also be appreciated that research cannot answer all questions. It can only study what is there, not what might be there if conditions changed. Analysis of the potential success of a new service which marks a radical departure from precedent poses a severe research problem. Research history is littered with examples of products and services which have succeeded despite the thumbs-down from the market analysts as well as products and services which have failed even though mountains of research have demonstrated that they would be successful. The study of existing requirements and attitudes towards services that are available may provide some clues, but will rarely do more than *indicate* whether a new service will receive the approval of customers. Market research is much happier with the study of 'what is' than with 'what might be'. Hypothetical questions receive hypothetical responses which may bear little resemblance to client practice once the new service is launched.

Some of the best marketing ideas have been suggested by good thinkers who have no direct marketing experience. There is always a need for inspiration and, when using market research, it is essential to concentrate on topics which respondents are capable of commenting on and also to know when to switch off the flow of facts and to concentrate on creativity.

Use of research by the professionals

To date, relatively few professions have made extensive use of market research. Small practices servicing narrow markets defined either by geography or specialised skill have rarely encountered sufficient direct or indirect competition to launch into marketing offensives demanding research backing. Many professions have been, or still are, prohibited from engaging in promotional activities, and this too has limited their thirst for information on the markets they service.

Over the last 5 years the pattern has altered. Liberalised by changes in attitude towards marketing by the controlling bodies of the professions, increasing numbers of the larger practices have initiated studies aimed at providing data to support their marketing and promotional campaigns. These have been both tactical exercises, designed to show what clients think of the services provided by the practices, as well as full strategic evaluations of markets designed to show sales potentials and diversification opportunities. The professions appear to be following the lead of providers of financial services, now some of the biggest spenders on market research, in appreciating that information-driven marketing programmes offer a better path to growth and profits.

METHODS OF DATA COLLECTION

To assess the usefulness of market research it is necessary to have some appreciation of how the data is collected. This section is not intended to provide a complete manual on how to undertake surveys, a need which is well catered for by other texts, but it is designed to provide the research user with some measure of confidence that the information is collected by techniques that give reliable and usable results. It is also designed to give enough insight into research methods to enable the professional to understand the researcher's jargon and contribute to important methodological decisions.

Research into professional markets can make use of three sources of data:

- published information
- information contained on data bases
- information collected directly from participants in the market.

Each of these can make a significant contribution to the understanding of a business, though the amount will vary from profession to profession.

Published information

'Secondary sources' commonly represent a rich source of information, and professional markets are no exception to this rule. Indeed the need to regulate professions by institutions, associations and government has resulted in an abundance of information which is of use to the market planner. Official sources of information are augmented by the output of other organisations that observe and report on the activities of the professions. These include:

- government statistics and reports
- directories and handbooks
- trade and professional magazines
- the national daily and weekly press
- the reports of general and specialist international bodies
- the reports and files of pressure and reform groups
- bank and stockbroker reports
- house magazines
- graduate theses
- seminar and conference papers
- the annual reports and accounts of limited companies.

There is considerable skill in identifying potential sources of useful information, and although the individual researcher can be assisted by numerous 'sources on sources', it can take some time to track down all that exists. Those with a 'nose' for sources know that there are always surprises – such as an item of information which is thought to be so obvious that it is bound to be available but proves to be completely elusive or the report of a little-known pressure group which contains a wealth of previously undisclosed facts about a business.

Published information is normally of most value in the following aspects of market assessment:

- the definition of the size of the current demand for the service
- past trends in demand for the service
- the performance of key customer groups
- targeting of individual potential customers
- descriptions of the structure of the profession and changes, such as mergers

- the identity of competitors, their size and background
- intelligence on the activities of competitors, including the acquisition or loss of important clients, new staff appointments and key staff losses
- the performance of competitors.

Government and professional association statistics may show total expenditure on a service, and there is invariably a considerable amount of other quantitative information which can be collected to provide a statistical profile of the market. This may include the number of active professionals, the number and regional locations of practices, sizes and specialisations of practices, the number of cases (projects) handled, project values and trends in activity over the recent past. The financial returns of those practices that have become limited companies can provide a clue to profitability and profit potential, though, obviously, where the partnership is the dominant organisational form, profitability cannot be examined directly.

Using published data effectively demands a skill in interpretation. Where information is not available directly, it can often be deduced with a reasonable level of confidence: for example, the number of active professionals multiplied by average revenues per professional may prove to be a perfectly adequate guide to industry and practice revenue, and information on staff movements can indicate success and failure, as can data on contracts won and lost.

Data bases

The professions have become used to data bases as a source of technical and case material, but they can also be a source of market information. In effect they are mechanised routes into published data, and the skills that have been developed in learning the protocols and interrogating the data bases can be turned to good use in market research. Many of the major statistical sources and news items are held on data bases and, although there are limits to usefulness created by the selective nature of the information contained, there is a trend for data bases to become increasingly comprehensive and therefore more valuable. The major data bases that carry information suitable for marketing purposes are Textline, Dialog, Infoline and Nexis.

Field research

The market-research activities which are most widely recognised are those devoted to the collection of primary information directly from participants in the market. The study of secondary sources is unlikely to reveal much qualitative information about the market-place, such as the conditions under which services are used and specified, the methods by which suppliers are identified, evaluated and selected, and the levels of client satisfaction with professional practices. For this information it is essential to talk directly to customers in a controlled manner which yields unbiased responses. It is also essential to talk to a cross-section of customers that can be deemed to be representative of the business as a whole, or at least that section of it in which the practice has a direct interest.

Respondents

Primary data can be collected from all participants in a market. The most common source of information is the client, who is obviously the prime target for marketing and promotional activity. However, it may also be essential to understand the opinions and practices of others, particularly where the services are being sold to business users rather than private customers. Typically these can include independent advisers who may influence supplier choice, intermediaries, such as agents, and even competitors. In the professions there are a number of incestuous relationships which may need to be explored, such as the role of the banks in recommending accountants and solicitors, and vice versa.

Questionnaires

Talking to respondents is undertaken by means of a questionnaire, which may be either fully structured, partially structured or completely open-ended. In a structured questionnaire all questions are set out together with the range of responses that are possible, including a 'don't know'. Such questionnaires are not difficult to administer and analyse but to compile them it is essential to know the range of responses that respondents may give. It is therefore common to commence a research programme with a limited number of what are described as 'in-depth'

Analysing the potential market

interviews, in which the interviewer uses a checklist of 'open-ended' questions and makes a verbatim record of the respondent's answers. These are used to understand the market-place and the variety and weight of the opinions that exist, and also to construct a structured questionnaire if some more broadly based quantification of factors is required, though it is entirely possible that the in-depth work will provide all the information that is needed. Semi-structured questionnaires, as their name implies, are a compromise between structured and open-ended questionnaires. The choice of questionnaire type depends entirely on the nature of the information to be collected, the types of respondents from which it is to be collected and the sample size to be covered.

Sampling

Nothing is more guaranteed to strike terror into the mind of the novice researcher than the prospect of sampling. It is indeed a complex subject, and sample error can be responsible for major inaccuracies in results. The user of research needs to be sure that the findings are based on reports from a sample which reflects the universe that is being reported on and not from a quirky sub-group that is totally unrepresentative. Daily exposure to the views of lobbyists who claim universal support for their opinions alerts us all to the dangers. Research therefore needs to demonstrate that the sample has been accurately drawn or, if there are limits imposed by the research approach, to state exactly what these are.

Samples may be drawn randomly or according to some form of quota. Truly random samples, in which any member of a universe has an equal chance of appearing, are rarely used, mainly because of difficulties in obtaining lists showing the composition of the universe and the adverse economics of having to interview anywhere in the country. It is common therefore to set quotas for specific groups of respondents, which can be defined by geography, socio-economic group or previous use of the service being studied. Where business use of the professional service is being studied, the quotas may be set according to activity, size of company and geographical location. Quotas are generally set according to some previous information on the structure of the universe gained by secondary research.

Sample sizes are generally dependent on the depth of analysis that is required. A detailed analysis of findings showing variations in opinion between user types will require a substantially larger sample than a global analysis of views and practices.

The sources of names for sampling require careful consideration. For some services, such as estate agents or banks, it is reasonable to assume that most individuals above a certain age will have made use of them. For others, such as divorce lawyers, it is not. Locating previous users of a service may therefore be a problem. In consumer work there is access to names drawn from the register of electors or telephone directories, but it is common to fill quotas by stopping individuals at random in pre-determined locations, and subjecting them to screening questions to identify their suitability. Client lists may be a useful source for part of a sample. Lists for business users may be available from general business directories, but screening to assess suitability is invariably required, since the lists rarely provide enough information to determine the precise use of services.

Interviewing

The administration of the questionnaire to the sample may be undertaken by personal or by telephone interviews. For more detailed examination of a problem, but with very limited samples, it is possible to make use of the group discussion, and in some work there is the possibility of using a questionnaire despatched and returned by mail.

Personal and telephone interviews are the most common forms of data collection. They can be applied with precision and the responses can be controlled during the progress of the interview. They are also more suited to sensitive subject matter, which could be the subject of professional service market examinations. The telephone has tended to become more popular for data collection largely because it is more cost-effective.

Group discussions, in which up to eight respondents are interviewed simultaneously, and therefore react to each others' views, is a technique which is used sparingly (because of the time and cost) but is invaluable for examinations in great depth. Postal questionnaires have some application in academic research or among special interest groups who have some incentive to respond, but are rarely used in commercial work. The main defect of the postal questionnaire is the inability of the researcher to control the response and thereby demonstrate that the results are representative.

Analysis

The critical stage in the research process is the analysis of the findings of the published and field research. Analysis techniques range from computer analysis of questionnaires to inspired interpretation using spreadsheets. However it is undertaken, it is essential that the results match the original objectives of the survey, and the researchers need to make frequent reference to the specification for the survey in order to ensure that the correct data are being produced. At the analysis stage it is essential to distinguish between useful and irrelevant data. The research process commonly throws up a considerable amount of data which cannot be acted upon and which therefore needs to be eliminated from the report or relegated to an appendix.

Analysis should extend to the research team's specifying its interpretation of the market situation that it has been responsible for studying, and providing the client with its views on the courses of action he should pursue. The views of the researchers will be subject to a number of limitations, but they will have a value, and the process of framing them will force the researchers to examine the completeness and usefulness of the data they have collected.

Reporting

Research results can be reported in the form of a written report and orally. It is common to do both. The submission of a written report followed by an oral presentation, which offers an opportunity for questions and answers, enables the research user to extract maximum benefit from his research budget. The questioning may raise the need for further analysis to supplement the initial report.

PROBLEMS ENCOUNTERED WHEN RESEARCHING PROFESSIONAL MARKETS

Researching professional markets is no more difficult than researching the markets for products. The lack of a tangible item affects the questions that are asked, but the success of manufacturing companies is determined as much by the service levels they provide as the products they offer, and researchers have long been used to analysing intangible benefits. Nevertheless, all markets have peculiarities which affect the research process and the availability of information, and professional businesses are subject to their fair share. The characteristics of professional markets which most affect research are listed below.

Sporadic and unpremeditated purchasing

Although many services, such as banking, are purchased in the same way as commodities, others are required infrequently (if ever), and the timing of demand may be dictated by events outside the control of the buyer. This means that the incidence of use is low and unforecastable. Furthermore, decision times can be too short for rational selection procedures to be undertaken. For effective market research it must be possible to identify respondents that have used a service, or are likely to use it, and to examine what they did. The character of the market may make both these requirements difficult.

Sensitivity of the services

Many services relate to subjects which are regarded as very personal, confidential and difficult to discuss. All discussions relating to finance, health, legal matters or death could encounter a high level of resistance, based on security, embarrassment or incomprehension. Researchers therefore need to find questioning methods which lower the barriers and encourage respondents to talk freely.

Professional's relationship with clients

The relationship between the client and the professional is such that the client may prove reluctant to discuss it or be unable to give any meaningful responses. Many users of services make a once-in-a-lifetime decision when selecting a supplier and, although professional markets are becoming more fluid, the loyalty of clients may be retained by little more than inertia and a feeling that professionals should not be treated in the same way as suppliers of fast-moving consumer goods. This will tend to exacerbate the difficulties of questioning, particularly with respect to competitor analysis, and result in a high proportion of 'don't know' responses.

Local markets

Some services are organised on a highly localised basis, and national market analysis is irrelevant. For these it is essential to confine surveys to the territory that is serviced by the supplier and to take full account of local market conditions.

Intangibility of the offer

The basis of the relationship between the professional and the client consists almost entirely of intangible factors, many of which cannot be quantified or duplicated. Long-standing relationships, family connections and track record with acquaintances serve to create trust and impose barriers to change. Although the factors can be understood, the knowledge is of marginal value in creating a competitive strategy. Research approaches need to be carefully tailored to avoid generating obvious and unusable information.

Organisational form

The predominance of the partnership in the professions means that financial information showing the performance of suppliers is scarcer than normal. The growth in the number of limited companies operating in the professions means that some information is available, but in the main this relates only to the larger practices, which are not typical for the business as a whole.

None of the above problems is insurmountable and may do little more than impose some methodological constraints on the research programme.

DATA COLLECTION SERVICES

All users of research have the option of collecting the information themselves or using the services of a professional research agency. Few companies have the resources to carry out large-scale research exercises and therefore turn to professional researchers for their information requirements. The case for using specialists is reinforced by the fact that research is required infrequently and is, in any event, best carried out anonymously by a team with no vested interest in the outcome.

Working with consultants can be a profitable experience, providing it is properly set up and monitored. The ground rules are simple:

- Provide the consultants with a thorough briefing on the nature of the marketing problem and the information which *you* feel is required to develop a solution.

- Indicate the data which are already available and which the research programme does not need to collect.

- Ask the consultants to prepare a proposal which specifies their understanding of the problem, the survey parameters, the information they propose to collect, the research methods they will use (including the number and type of interviews), the time the survey will take and the cost.

- Determine whether the fee is fixed or whether there are escalation factors, and, if so, what they are for.

- Meet the research team that will be assigned to the project if you proceed.

- Once commissioned, meet the team at appropriate intervals to monitor progress and discuss possible changes.

- Make sure you receive a full written and oral presentation of research findings, complete with recommended courses of action to solve the problem.

The needs of a small local practice may not justify the employment of a research consultancy, but it too is unlikely to have either the time or the expertise to undertake a survey itself. There are some alternative methods of obtaining information which can be considered. The United Kingdom has a considerable resource of freelance consultants who act for individual clients and whose fee rates are likely to be lower than full service consultancies. The marketing departments of many technical colleges and universities undertake projects for outside clients as an exercise for students; both charge fees and, under pressure from the University Grants Committee, these have tended to escalate, but they may still offer good value compared to consultancies. Finally, those that are more confident in their abilities to specify and control a research project can consider employing students direct, both to collect information and analyse the findings.

THE VALUE OF RESEARCH

Marketers, who fully understand the need for information in order to formulate their strategies, rarely have doubts about commissioning a research programme. To them, information is a commodity having a value that makes it worth acquiring. The professional practice approaching marketing for the first time will need to be convinced that data are worth the cost of acquisition. It is of course possible that a measure of scepticism is justified, and before embarking on a research exercise the professional should ask himself and his research advisers a series of simple questions in order to determine whether the research budget will be wisely spent:

- What is the nature of the marketing problem faced?
- What, if any, data will help me solve the marketing problem?
- Can market-research techniques obtain reliable information on the market?
- What is the cost of acquiring the data?
- Are there alternative and less costly means of acquiring the information?
- What is the level of risk surrounding the decision?
- What is at stake if the wrong decision is made?
- Will the information be fully used in the decision-making process?
- Do I have the resources to implement the strategies suggested by the research findings?

Research can only be regarded as worthwhile if it contributes to making correct decisions, the results are implemented to the benefit of the practice and the cost of acquiring the information is less than the contribution it makes to profit performance. Under these circumstances research can demonstrate a pay-off and is worth undertaking.

CONCLUSION

Information is a vital component of the marketing process and is as important to professions as it is to those marketing consumer and industrial products. Without data there is a risk that marketing strategies will be inappropriate. Market research uses a rigorous set of techniques to collect information but is not the sole source. The markets for professional services have some peculiarities that can frustrate the research process, but these are not insurmountable. Before committing oneself to a research programme, it is worth talking to a research consultant to discuss the problem, the contribution that research can make to its solution and the likely order of cost. If it appears that research can make a cost-effective contribution to a strategy that will create a competitive advantage, then solicit firm proposals.

FURTHER READING

Connor, Richard and Davidson, Jeffrey *Marketing Your Consulting and Professional Practice* (John Wiley, New York, 1985)

Hague, Paul *The Industrial Market Research Handbook* (Kogan Page, 1985)

Wilson, Aubrey *The Marketing of Professional Services* (McGraw-Hill, 1972), ch. 8

Wilson, Aubrey *The Assessment of Industrial Markets* (Associated Business Publications, 1973)

Worcester, Robert and Downham, John (eds.) *Consumer Market Research Handbook*, Third Edition (McGraw-Hill, 1986)

5

ANALYSING STRENGTHS AND WEAKNESSES
by Ian R. Brown

EDITORS' PREVIEW

Ian Brown, MSc, BIM, MCIM, is a faculty course director of the Chartered Institute of Marketing, College of Marketing. A former lecturer at the Bristol Polytechnic and at the Universities of Bath and Bristol, he is now the proprietor of Marketing Decisions, a marketing research consultancy in Bristol, and has specialised in the marketing of services.

The honest appraisal of the strengths and weaknesses of one's own company is, in many cases, the most critical and difficult task, particularly in a partnership environment. In the more normal commercial, pyramidal structure it is much easier. But in a partnership, particularly one in which partners specialise in the offering of specific elements of the services, self-analysis can present a problem.

Ian Brown has set out some simple guidelines on ways of approaching this delicate matter.

MAKING AN HONEST APPRAISAL

Within the constraints set by the market, what is actually achieved by any business will very much depend on the quality and quantity of resources available, and how these resources are organised. This is particularly true for a firm dealing in intellectual property, where what the customer buys cannot be stored, is difficult to sample or have demonstrated, cannot be resold, and where production is often seen as a quasi-social process in which the customer often participates quite closely.

'Professional advice' comes at the end of the service spectrum (see Figure 5.1) and is about the most difficult 'product' to market well. What professional advisers are providing, for which they hope customers will pay, is of its very nature:

- INTANGIBLE
- INSEPARABLE from the people providing the advice.
- HETEROGENEOUS, in that the customers' perceptions of the quality of the advice are coloured by their perception of the person providing it.
- PERISHABLE
- DIFFICULT TO OWN
- COLOURED BY OTHER CUSTOMERS (and their reactions) – who they are and how they are perceived.
- COLOURED BY THE PROCESS in which the advice is produced, presented and delivered.

Professional advisers therefore need to counter where necessary, and exploit where possible, the fundamental differences between what they take to market and what is marketed by, say, a manufacturer of such goods as toothpaste, TVs or motor cars. These differences will require a fundamentally different approach to marketing.

Successful strategies will build and exploit an image of the firm, a concept which has even more value today than did Shakespeare's 'the bubble reputation', which we seek 'even in the cannon's mouth'; and over and above the classic marketing mix of

PRODUCT

PRICE

PLACE (distribution)

PROMOTION

the professional adviser must take stock of, and use wisely, the resources of

PHYSICAL EVIDENCE

PEOPLE

PROCESS

PRESENTATION

Before any strategy or plan be formulated, it is wise to appraise the firm's strengths and weaknesses – in other words, to define its competence profile. The appraisal, however, needs to take place against a framework of understanding of what it is that makes this type of business so different to market.

THE NATURE OF A PROFESSIONAL SERVICE BUSINESS

Professional advice shares a great deal in common with other services. The service spectrum ranges at the one end from consumer services such as 'fast food' to professional advice and consultancy at the other. The relevant importance of these differences, and how the marketing mix must alter to accommodate and/or exploit them, will vary according to where on this spectrum the 'service' in question is placed.

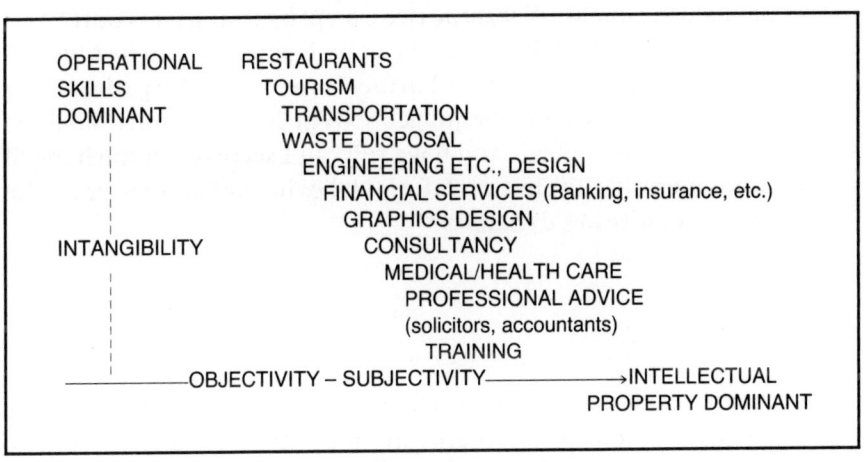

```
OPERATIONAL      RESTAURANTS
SKILLS           TOURISM
DOMINANT         TRANSPORTATION
                   WASTE DISPOSAL
                     ENGINEERING ETC., DESIGN
                       FINANCIAL SERVICES (Banking, insurance, etc.)
                         GRAPHICS DESIGN
INTANGIBILITY            CONSULTANCY
                         MEDICAL/HEALTH CARE
                           PROFESSIONAL ADVICE
                           (solicitors, accountants)
                             TRAINING
         ────OBJECTIVITY – SUBJECTIVITY─────────→INTELLECTUAL
                                                 PROPERTY DOMINANT
```

FIGURE 5.1 The services spectrum

Intangibility

Just as the essential quality of a good is its tangibility, so that of a service is its intangibility. Whereas goods are produced, services are performed. One cannot therefore touch, taste, smell or weigh a service.

Intangibility inhibits objective measurement, and, just as it is the variation in the wavelength of light that determines where one finds what colour on the visible spectrum, so it is the variation in the degree to which one can objectively judge the 'quality' of a service which gives dimension to the service spectrum. See Figure 5.1.

For services at the top left-hand of the figure there are inherent factors that enable one to judge quality:

- the furnishing of a room
- the speed of waiter service
- the comfort of the furniture
- the glamour of the resort
- the age of the aeroplanes chartered
- the state of repair, cleanliness, etc. of the accommodation.

But in the bottom right-hand corner, judgement is not so easy. How can a layman judge the quality of legal advice except by taking it to court? And if we lose our case at law, how much can be blamed on the bad luck of drawing an unsympathetic judge? Furthermore, the quality of training (say in software use) cannot be judged except by the results obtained when that training is applied. And if we still can't seem to get the hang of that new programme, how much of the fault lies in our failure to grasp the subtleties of the software dynamics?

Physical evidence

The very intangibility at the heart of any service, its invisibility, leads to the first extra element of the marketing mix for services. The need to 'tangibilise' the service, to render it visible, leads to the adoption of some form of *physical evidence* as a sign of the service, a sort of surrogate via which the service can be judged.

Examples of physical evidence are often part and parcel of the services at the top end of our spectrum, and have been cited as examples above (re restaurants, airlines, etc.). At the 'intellectual property' end of the spectrum, the wise marketer will exploit and emphasise physical evidence often quite blatantly, so that the consultant will wear high-quality clothing such as Savile Row suits, tailored shirts and ties, and will sport custom-made shoes, briefcase etc. He will probably drive an automobile that similarly expresses the consultancy's position in the market.

Should clients have need to call on him, his offices can similarly be used to communicate success, and should therefore be chosen with care, be well designed and well decorated internally and externally. They should ideally be located in an appropriate area of town.

If the advice is given in any other location, this location should be chosen with care so that it gives the right message. The value of advice given to clients in a plush hotel may be no more than advice that may be given in a scout hut, but clients will invariably be more receptive in the former than the latter.

People

Businesses providing professional advice, in common with most service businesses, are almost invariably people businesses. The proportion of employees in such a business who regularly meet customers face to face, or on the telephone, as part of their job is almost the exact mirror-image of the proportion who would regularly meet customers if that firm were producing goods. In the latter case about 10 per cent of the workforce would meet customers and 90 per cent would not, whereas professional advisers should expect that up to 90 per cent of their employees will regularly meet customers and less than 10 per cent will never do so.

Inseparability

People are more often than not *inseparable* from professional advice. We can therefore usefully add value to the service provided by considering it as a double-sided coin – on one side the 'material' aspects of the service, and on the other the 'interpersonal' aspects.

Amongst much else the material aspects included are such factors as:

- speed of answering the telephone in an office
- speed of fulfilling the promise of a proposed oral report
- hours when available for consultation
- clarity of language and presentation of facts, etc.

As regards the interpersonal aspects, every time a customer meets a service provider, the firm is on trial. How that service provider performs determines the way the service is perceived.

Jan Carlzon of Scandinavian Airlines System calls this customer–provider contact *a moment of truth*.

Boiled down simply, it is the degree to which those *serving* are able to make each customer feel:

- well served
- that the business values their custom
- that they want to do their business with the firm again.

Material and interpersonal aspects are inseparable, the performance of the former often being the only means of measuring the commitment of those providing the service. (The training and maintenance of interpersonal skills, as a part of service marketing policy, often goes under the label of 'customer care'.)

Customer care

Customer care training, however, is only one part of the story; it should not be viewed as only the concern of those in contact with the customers. If customer care is to be a useful part of the way the firm does business, then it must become a total management philosophy, complete with feedback systems to monitor performance and maintain standards through appropriate training, incentive and disciplinary measures. To quote Jan Carlzon again, 'Those who are not serving customers should make sure that they are serving those who are.'

The quality of any business's customer care is determined by sound relevant policies for such aspects as:

1 *Recruitment.* All people in the firm should be chosen with care, be they associates or receptionists. Some people are naturals at human relations; others have to be trained in order to realise their potential. A surprising number of people have an unsuitable personality (e.g. introverted/shy or ingrained superiority or inferiority complexes). Principals take heed!
2 *Management.* 'To give of their best, those meeting customers need to be managed well and appropriately' (C. Handy[1]). Good management includes good 'continual training' policies and practices, and appropriate motivation strategies.
3 *Empowerment.* As one moves across the service spectrum, so the importance of this aspect grows. Empowerment is to do with the degree to which the service provider has the authority and power to use his or her initiative when dealing with customers. The more the business is to the right of the spectrum, then the more important it is that those in contact with customers should have the power, the ability, the willingness *and* the training to use their initiative in the furtherance of the business.

Homogeneity

All people are not the same. In the unlikely event of all else being equal, the same service provided by two people to the same material *and* interpersonal standard will still be perceived differently by the same customer. Two different customers will hold different views as to the quality of service delivered, though of the same material and interpersonal standard, from the same service provider.

Thus not only are services inseparable from people by their very nature, but they inevitably vary in perceived quality from one person to another. In fact they are heterogeneous in delivery.

For the marketer this is either a liability or an asset, depending on the firm's position in the spectrum. The more that intellectual property is part of the service, the greater is the influence of an individual's personality on the way the service is provided and on its perceived quality.

At this end of the spectrum customers 'buy their perceptions of the people' in the expectation that good people will provide good service. In this sense particularly, *the people are the service*. The more the firm is to the right of the service spectrum, the more this phenomenon can be exploited to advantage.

Customers tend to be handled more on a one-to-one basis the further right of this spectrum one goes. Where the value of business from customers is high enough, the favourite strategy is to select service providers who are congruent and acceptable to the customer – a horses-for-courses or an 'account handler' policy. Thus conservative City gents in blue pinstripe suits are most suitably looked after by sober-suited people apparently from the same social and educational strata if not milieu. On the other hand, a young, trendy producer of pop records should be looked after by an equally trendy young person.

This is not an invariable rule; it can be broken to good effect where the situation demands. The City gent may not believe the person he meets to be sufficiently creative if he/she does not look the part. Similarly the successful record producer will be wary of accepting investment advice from a hippy – no matter how trendy.

Lower down the firm, the people providing the administrative and support services within the organisation cannot be so 'type-cast' and other policies may have to be employed.

If the firm can afford to hire the best people, it should do so; their commitment to the firm and what it is trying to achieve is valuable at whatever level. How your people dress and how they deal with clients and potential clients have a powerful influence on your firm's image.

If, for reasons of the local labour market, etc., it is not possible to hire such committed people, then some element of regimentation may be necessary. For example, it may be necessary to specify those who are allowed to come into contact with clients, and under what circumstances, and perhaps even staff office uniform may be necessary to ensure a consistent standard of dress.

Perishability

Services, because they are performed, are perishable. They cannot be produced for stock in quiet times, to be sold when business picks up later on.

Services are performed via resources such as people and/or capital equipment. The extent of the resources at the firm's disposal determines the volume of business that can be done over any given time. Indeed professional advisers can often usefully be viewed as selling the availability/use of their resources over time, such that lawyers charge by the hour, consultants by the day. The raw demand for any service is rarely ever a smooth line.

Expressed demand is often the result of an harmonic of many cycles, such as the seasons, the economy, fashion trends, etc. Thus the professional adviser shares the dilemma central to the resourcing and pricing strategies of marketing any service. *Does the business gear up to be able to handle peak demand, or does it economise on resources so that it is only comfortable during 'normal' demand?*

At one extreme the strategy might be to provide sufficient resources to be able to handle peak demand without flinching, but even a crude Pareto analysis will show that peak demand will only exist for about 20 per cent of the time; thus for the remaining 80 per cent of the time any firm adopting this strategy will have resources, people and capital equipment surplus to its needs.

Spare capacity still costs money: people have to be paid, even though it may be a 'basic' or a 'retainer' and equipment will still depreciate and/or its leasing costs will have to be met, used or not. But there are few things worth less than unsold time past – the lawyer that did no work for a client on Tuesday cannot sell Tuesday's time on Wednesday. On Wednesday he can only perform Wednesday's work and sell the time to come, he cannot sell one second of time past.

So spare capacity is an unproductive overhead that can only be supported by the income produced by those resources in use. This of necessity predicates a high price policy. How else can one part of the business support the other?

The diametric opposite of a strategy for peak demand is to provide resources sufficient only to cope with 'normal' demand – a *modus operandi* most often found in firms that adopt a so-called operations orientation. Just enough resources are provided to be able to handle the 80 per cent of occasions when demand is off-peak. The consequence of this is that during the remaining 20 per cent of time, when demand peaks, there is an increased probability of several undesirable eventualities, with the inevitable outcome of a greatly increased risk of losing customers.

Overstretched resources almost inevitably lead to a deterioration of the quality of total service provided, if not the actual 'advice' itself, often for some time afterwards. People get tired and start making more mistakes, they inevitably give less personal attention, they fail to anticipate, etc., and it may take a while after the peak for them to recover.

Capital equipment designed to run 12 hours a day starts to malfunction if run for 20 hours continuously for too many consecutive days. Downtime for the consequent increased maintenance, or even breakdowns, serves to exacerbate the situation.

Sub-contracting, or hiring in short-term associates, if that is possible, will not completely solve the situation. In the first case the firm loses control over the quality of the total service, including the advice, unless a great deal of care is taken in supervision. (And what's to say that supervisory resources are infinitely stretchable?) In the second case short-term people will require extra supervision, and unless one is extremely lucky, will inevitably lack the level of commitment and expertise of the regular team.

There are exceptions to this rule but the rule holds good nevertheless.

When capacity is fully booked and regular customers are asked to queue, the risk of competitors getting a toe-hold in the business increases alarmingly. If they are then well served by competitors, why then should these customers ever return? Thus a strategy of minimum resourcing will inevitably lead to minimal pricing and a high risk of customer turnover, which tends to encourage still lower prices, all leading to so-called commodity trading and the leanest of margins.

The only sure strategy to deal with the perishability problem is diversification of some sort. The key is to identify other uses to which the firm's resources can be put when the main profit-earning business is off-peak. For example, a market-research firm could perhaps use its computers off-peak as a word-processing/data-processing bureau, as could other firms, such as accountants, management consultants, loss assessors, surveyors, etc., where there is the need for similar word-processing hardware.

The problem with this strategy is that the further on the service spectrum one goes towards intellectual property, the more constrained one becomes by the degree of specialisation necessary. What does a firm of solicitors do in times of slack demand, or an architect do between projects?

Ownership

For the professional adviser the main aspect of this phenomenon is the ownership of the idea, the intellectual property lying at the root of the service. To all intents and purposes one cannot patent the intellectual property behind professional advice.

The inventor of the safety pin was able to profit from the innovation because firms had to pay him for the right to manufacture. No firm may produce window glazing via the float glass process unless they pay a licence fee and a royalty to Pilkingtons.

But who owns the idea of a 'charge card'? Any financial institution, given compliance with appropriate legislation, is free to launch its own. A consultant, an accountant, a lawyer, or a freelance trainer has few rights over the intellectual property of his advice. Plagiarism not withstanding, the idea at the heart of such a service cannot be protected in the same way as a good can be patented.

This aspect of service marketing leads to many classic dilemmas. The very acts of consulting, training, publishing, promoting, put the idea, if not the method of execution, into the public domain, from which all who wish can draw practical inspiration for their business. The means of coping with this aspect of marketing a service are many, but boil down to a strategy of differentiation of one sort or another.

With proper care one can protect a trading name, the service equivalent of a brand. With determination and thoroughness one can establish a unique corporate image.[2]

Businesses providing a service must take care to provide customers with a sound set of hygiene factors (re F. H. Hertzberg) in terms of the quality of the performance of their service. But on its own this is not enough. *Motivational* factors must also be supplied to customers. Such factors are reasons why the customer should buy from *you* rather than from the competition. This is a *key strategic concept*, the competitive *differential* about which we have more to say later in this chapter (see 'The service promise', p. 79).

Effort must therefore be spent identifying what is, or is to be, the firm's competitive differential. The aim is that, within the constraints of professional ethics, the firm must flaunt its differential, if it has one; if not, then no effort must be spared in acquiring one.

Intercustomer influence

This aspect of a professional adviser's business is both part of the 'product' and an essential part of its 'promotion'. Perhaps the best example in the service sector of this aspect being part of the 'product' is in the restaurant business.

Only few customers go to a restaurant just for the quality of the food. For success, a restaurateur must treat the 'product' as a total experience, in which the food plays only a part. The restaurant's location, its external *and* internal decor, the interpersonal skills of the staff are all of equal importance to create the right ambience. But the most powerful contributor to this ambience is the other customers who are present at the time.

This is as strong an influence in most people's choice of professional adviser, as it is in their choice of restaurant, their holiday destination, mode of travel, evening's entertainment (theatre vs cinema vs pub vs club vs disco, etc.), even perhaps political party. They will be influenced by their view of the 'type' of people, their dress, their manners, their speech, who will either be present at the time, or who are known to deal with that firm. At the very least customers will feel most comfortable among those people they consider to be their own kind, or those in whose company, even indirectly, they will feel the most at ease.

Thus customers are an indispensable part of many service products, not least professional advice. Their presence is an essential benefit, and hence an attraction.

Customers are also vital to the promotion of professional advice in another way. It is often difficult if not impossible to sample a service, and at the start of any relationship customers often buy no more than the promise of good service. This becomes an acute issue the more the business in point is positioned towards the intellectual property end of the service spectrum.

Potential customers will be hungry for clues as to reasons to buy, and the absence of appropriate clues will tend to deter purchase. 'Corporate image', 'physical evidence', 'location', the quality of the 'people', will all influence the decision to buy.

In such situations the firm's 'client list' acts as sampling by proxy; the implication is that 'if this service is good enough for so-and-so, it should be good enough for you', viz., an implied endorsement. Client lists therefore are truly the professional adviser's equivalent of an army regiment's battle honours.

Take care, however. In the same way that we may not wish to visit those pubs frequented by people in whose company we could feel uncomfortable, for whatever reason, so customers can be deterred from using our services by clients with whom they may not wish to associate. So if you deal heavily with Israeli firms, don't bother trying to attract too many firms from Arab countries, and if you have a strong South African client base, forget Black Africa. If your firm provides legal advice to squatters and drug addicts, don't expect too many landlords or fathers with young families to be too happy dealing with you.

Performance is central to marketing

The effort put into the performance of a given service must be viewed as at least equal to the effort put into the rest of its marketing. For example, waiters, trainers, consultants, barristers, travel couriers, even barmen are all selling the service in the very act of its production. So good service from them is vital.

The first duty of any service provider is to sell more service, but the only way a service business can grow is to add *and keep* new customers. Getting the customer in the first instance is relatively easy; it's keeping customers coming back for more that is the hard part. Even for services which by their nature may enjoy very little repeat business, such as barristers, surgeons, estate agents, or undertakers (*in extremis* you can still only be cremated once), good service gains satisfied customers, and these are your best advocates.

The disadvantage of long-term relationships with customers is that the situation can so easily lead to complacency unless strict management systems are in place to avoid this happening. Over time, unless guarded against, the standard of service will deteriorate and customers will not be made aware of how poor the service has become until a competitor gets a chance to serve them well. That customer may never return.

Process

The third extra element to the marketing mix for a service is therefore the 'process' – the way in which the professional advice is delivered. The delivery system itself must be:

- Well in place – the firm must be able to deliver the service and to the standard promised. A dissatisfied customer is perhaps more potent than a satisfied customer but they work to turn others away.

- Exploited to the full if capable of impressing customers (or well hidden if not).

There is a saying – 'Sell the sizzle not the steak'. The marketer of professional advice must be concerned to sell the sizzle *and* the steak.[3]

If the service can be delivered or performed with style, perhaps with panache, then do so – such a policy can be a potent form of differentiation. Ask any successful barrister. Each business providing a service should do its equivalent of broiling the steaks in the window, whirling the pizza bread for all to see, and serving 'à la flambée' at the table. Inject (the right level of) showmanship whenever and wherever possible.

But, as the Scots say, 'Ne'er show an infant or a fool a job half done'. If your service is delivered via a process that is incomprehensible to customers, and, worse still, unimpressive, don't let customers anywhere near.

Few people understand what is happening on the trading floor of a commodities exchange, or in a bank's foreign exchange dealing room, but most are impressed nonetheless. If your service is like that, exploit it.

Still fewer people can understand the process of computer software creation, tax computations, or seeking legal precedent, and because such work mainly goes on in people's heads, and is therefore truly invisible, only the *cognoscente* can be impressed. If your process is similar to the latter, keep customers and the process far apart.

The service triangle

Another perspective which provides a useful framework for an analysis of strengths and weaknesses is that of the service triangle, which we depict in Figure 5.2. The service 'product' must be seen as a triangle with the customer at the centre of gravity. The service operation may be compared to a three-legged milking stool. Take one leg away, and the stool falls over.

Each of the three points of the triangle is defined as follows.

Analysing strengths and weaknesses

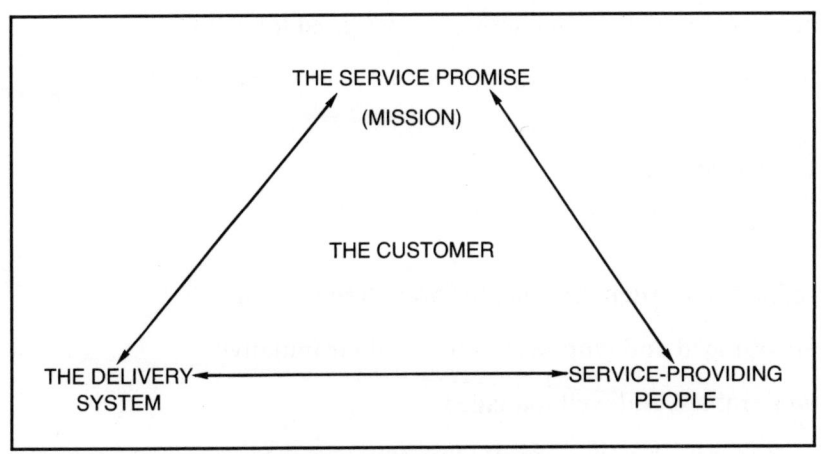

FIGURE 5.2 The service triangle

The service promise

Sometimes called the mission statement, the promise should be:

- a non-trivial statement of intent
- the competitive differential expressed
- something of *real value* to the target group of customers, i.e. they will pay extra for it, and/or be prepared to go out of their way to gain access
- Deliverable.

The mission is the yardstick for decision-taking. Having a 'mission', however, is only part of the story; it must also be *communicated* to employees *and* customers alike.

The delivery system

The delivery system should be:

- based on the 'mission'
- customer- *and* employee-friendly, i.e. easy to understand and operate rather than designed for the convenience of the administration

- possessed of a 'feedback loop', i.e. designed for self-correction
- Invisible in normal operation, i.e. only seen when it goes wrong.

Service-providing people

These people should be:

- recruited for their aptitude for providing a service
- encouraged and empowered to use their initiative
- well trained and well managed
- well aware of, and committed to, the service 'mission' (the promise)
- set, and be aware of, goals and performance expectations
- kept informed as to their performance
- appropriately rewarded with attention, recognition *and* money
- well supported by management from the top of the organisation down.

The executive multiplier

This concept has a direct bearing on the long-term profitability of a firm providing professional advice. Well exploited, the concept multiplies the earning power of each executive day by ensuring that as often as is possible executive days are sold as part of a total package of ancillary services, each part of which earns a profit in its own right.

The nature of businesses based on intellectual property is such that in a very real sense the principals *are the firm*; the rest of the organisation is the means by which the principals' expertise is delivered to the market. Put another way, the firm exists to better express the entrepreneurial flair of the principals. Therefore, in the same way that the mechanical machine helps magnify man's muscle, and the personal computer (PC) magnifies the intellect, thus a firm should be organised so as to magnify its principals' ability to do business.

At a basic level, there are some activities and professions that inevitably confine the professional adviser; Barristers may only be in one court at a time, training consultants leading a seminar may be nowhere else. These are unmultiplied days in that the consultant days taken up by these activities are usually devoid of other profit-earning services and of the ability to keep other people in the firm directly employed. But what if the marketing consultant were to sell market-research services as well? One executive day designing, supervising or analysing research would also lead to time being spent by fieldworkers, interviewers, data specialists, etc., all of which can be sold at a profit in addition to the basic executive day.

The temptation to do just one's own thing, particularly in a smaller practice, also leads to excessive incipient instability in that the livelihood of everyone else in the firm depends solely on the executive days sold. If the principal in question is taken ill, or otherwise is unable to contribute directly, then everything else can easily collapse.

Analysis and pre-strategy formulation should therefore examine what potential exists for executive multiplier activity for your firm.

HOW TO GATHER THE INFORMATION

Issues like the executive multiplier and deciding on what should be your firm's best levels for resourcing are matters for constructive internal reflection and perhaps a brainstorming session rather than formal research. However, matters such as the appropriateness of the people employed and their customer contact/core aptitudes and skills, and employees' attitudes toward the customer and the firm, are issues that require to be addressed formally.

The exercise falls naturally into two parts, the external and the internal studies.

External studies

External studies to assess the competence profile of the firm are often known as the 'Image Audit' or market attitude and opinion surveys. These activities are too important to be handled by amateurs or treated as 'one-off' exercises.

Even though the professional practice may be small and the funds not available for a full study, a marketing research consultant agency should be engaged to oversee the design of the questionnaire and analyse the results. Ideally the external exercise should be carried out by an objective, disinterested outsider, and if professional market researchers are used, the name of the client firm, your practice, can be kept confidential, thus reducing the likelihood that respondents will use the research as a channel of communication specifically back to you.

Such a study should focus along the lines discussed above, on the perceptions that customers, potential customers, their influences, validators and other important members of their respective decision-making unit (DMU) have of the practice, and how they compare it with your competition. It will be important to let these respondents define who the competitors are; one can often be surprised by who customers consider them to be.

Apart from gathering information to act as the basis for strategy formulation, the external exercise will set the datum against which the degree of success of future marketing action can be measured objectively. Thus, in perhaps a truncated form, the exercise should be repeated on some regular basis, at least once a year, depending on the size of the practice.

Internal studies

Since professional advice is about people, the perceptions, attitudes and opinions of employees towards their firm are a critical issue. How they feel about the company will rub off on customers, because it will unavoidably colour the way your people behave toward them. Happy employees, with the right skills, create positive perceptions about the firm; unhappy employees can sabotage the pay-off from all other marketing activity.

Staying in touch with employee attitudes should be no problem for the small practice if well managed. 'Management by walking about' ('one minute' style) should provide all that the principals need to know.

The problems come with the larger practices, such as are found in the professions of consultant engineering, quantity surveying, accountancy, and financial services. Here firms can be so large and dispersed that the only practical way to gather and to monitor this aspect of the company's competence profile is regularly to administer and analyse the results of an internal staff questionnaire.

It is best that this study be completed by staff anonymously, in order to prevent them being inhibited in what they say. On this issue of inhibition, it is also found best to have the study expedited by an outside body such as a marketing-research firm. Staff fill in their individual questionnaires and post them back directly to the outsider, thus ensuring full confidentiality of their replies.

REFERENCES

1 Handy, C. *The Gods of Management* (Pan)
2 Olins, Wally *Corporate Identity: the Myth and the Reality* (Thames & Hudson, 1989)
3 *Ibid.*

6

CREATING THE BUSINESS PLAN
by Geoffrey Randall

EDITORS' PREVIEW

Geoffrey Randall, MA, a graduate of the University of Oxford, is currently an independent consultant. He was formerly dean of the Faculty of Business, Social Sciences and Humanities, and head of the Business School at Thames Polytechnic. He is also a past governor of the CAM Foundation and a member of the National Marketing Education Board. He is author of a number of publications, including *Managing New Products*, which is published by the British Institute of Management, and a forthcoming book on trade marketing to be published by Heinemann.

Following on from the previous two chapters, in which the need to analyse the market-place and examine internal strengths and weaknesses has been stressed, we now come to the task of creating a full business plan. Geoffrey Randall makes the point that planning is not to impose restrictions, 'but to prevent a firm growing in a lopsided way and getting unbalanced'. Also analysed is the way in which the changing structure of the population will affect professional practices in the mid-1990s.

WHY PLAN?

Planning is one of those management techniques which appeared to have its own product life cycle. In the 1960s it was heavily promoted, and corporate planning – with its apparatus of highly paid central planners and tortuous jargon – was adopted by many companies. Like so many miracle techniques, it was over-sold, and was not the panacea for all ills. Not surprisingly, many people rejected it (some after difficult experiences with it, some without trying it at all). Cynics were ready to pronounce it dead.

This is to mistake the mystique for the reality. As General Eisenhower said, 'Planning is everything; the plan is nothing'. What planning is about is control of our own destiny. The one thing we know for certain is that life around us will change; unless we are ready for it, change will stop us doing what we want to, perhaps even by putting us out of business. Therefore we need to look ahead and plot our course.

For professional service firms the idea of control is particularly sensitive. Often the partners are specialists in their own fields, and their value lies in their ability to capitalise on their skills and reputation. They are necessarily entrepreneurial, and the idea of *control* seems limiting. The point of planning in such circumstances is not to impose restrictions, but to prevent the firm growing in a lopsided way and getting unbalanced.

The other compelling reason for planning is lead time. Professional advisers are not like some industries, such as power generation, which count their lead time in decades, or motor manufacturers, who plan production facilities 5 years ahead. They do, however, have lead times to think about. Consider their main asset – people.

Between the late 1980s and the mid-1990s the size of the school/higher education leaver group in Britain will fall by some 25 per cent. As the demand for graduates is rising, one employer has estimated that the shortfall will be 40 per cent. If a firm relies on highly educated staff, it needs to plan now for this situation, as it will not be able to go on recruiting as it has in the past. New strategies will be needed: e.g. training less-qualified entrants, using part-time staff, such as young mothers, retaining older people as consultants.

THE PLANNING PROCESS

Accepting the need to plan ahead, we may also accept that the old, complicated processes are not suitable. The planning process can be reduced to answering a few basic questions:

Creating the business plan

- What will happen around us to affect our business?
- Who are we?
- Who do we want to be?
- Where are we now?
- Where do we want to be?
- How shall we get there?

The reason that planning seems (and *is*) difficult is that these questions are simple to ask but not to answer. They interact, so that the process becomes *iterative*. Answers to later questions affect the answers to earlier ones, so that we have to make several passes through the cycle, making adjustments each time.

The messy reality as opposed to the neat theory is that there is no one answer to the question as to whether planning should be top-down or bottom-up: it must be both. Top management must set objectives, but may have to revise these in the light of detailed market assessments in one department. A section of the business may have to go back to the drawing-board to replan when downstream decisions are made, for example on premises available.

The aim should be that those managing the business think through the basic decisions which will affect the business over the years to come, that the implications of these decisions are worked out, and that the results of the planning process are communicated to those who will have to carry out the plan. The effect of planning should be to give focus to the firm's activities, and to allow it to respond to change and meet new challenges.

THE PLANNING CYCLE

Devising a plan for a firm is not a one-off action; the process should be seen as continuous. Typically a business plan will contain a detailed 1-year plan and an increasingly broad outline for the following 4 years. Working back from the beginning of any one year, therefore, it is clear that the plan needs to be finalised and agreed 2 or 3 months from year-end. Working back from that, the whole process will spread over almost the whole year, with preliminary work for next year starting soon after the beginning of this year's operations. Quite how long and complicated the process is will depend on the size and nature of the organisation, but it will always be overlapping and cyclical.

A typical cycle might be:

February–March	Environmental scan carried out and communicated to top management and operating units
April–May	A statement of business or commercial philosophy and long-range objectives formulated, discussed and revised
June–July	Operating unit outline 5-year plans designed and consolidated; objectives revised
September	Operating unit 1-year plans drawn up
October	1-year plans reviewed, revised and consolidated.

When the system is working fully, a parallel review of this year's operations will be going on, and will itself contribute to the planning, particularly of next year.

The stages will now be considered in more detail.

SCANNING THE ENVIRONMENT

The pace and impact of change in our world means that managers must lift their eyes from the details of their business now, and spend some of their time looking at a wider horizon. They need to speculate on what forces will affect their business in 5 years' time, and what will affect their clients' businesses.

These forces are not only *economic*, although for many people these will be the most important. The other influences to be examined will vary from business to business, but may include:

- SOCIAL   How is society changing in its structure, habits, attitudes, needs?

Creating the business plan

- POLITICAL   Will the political climate continue in its present direction, or will there be a reaction? What would be the impact of such a change?

- LEGAL   What legislative changes may occur, both at national and supra-national level (e.g. EEC law)? Will our profession be deregulated, or subject to much tighter control?

- TECHNOLOGICAL   How will emerging technologies (IT, bio-technology, flexible manufacturing, new materials, superconductivity, etc.) impact on all the businesses with which we deal directly or indirectly?

- INDUSTRY STRUCTURE   As a result of the changes forecast, what will happen to the industries which concern us, nationally and internationally? Will old industries die and new ones be born? Will new competitors appear, and from where?

Obviously there is a high degree of uncertainty in peering into the future, and an infinite number of combinations of outcomes. One way of dealing with this complexity is by using *scenarios*. A scenario is a description of a particular set of future developments which may affect a business. The technique was pioneered by Shell: for example, the company's planners asked managers when the price of oil was $30 a barrel to say how they would manage in a world in which the price was $15 a barrel. The managers were reluctant, since they felt the scenario was completely unrealistic, but they carried out the exercise. Thus, when the price was actually $13 a barrel, they could cope.

Although the world of Shell is very different from that of most firms of professional advisers, the technique can be applied just as well to small firms as to large, and to services as to manufacturing. A group of managers can brainstorm possible futures, perhaps helped by an outside expert, or by younger members of the firm who are less constrained by experience and more in touch with trends.

For example, a firm of consulting engineers with a worldwide practice might generate the following scenario:

Orders from the Middle East dry up; competition from Pacific Rim countries grows, with an emphasis on low price, clients become increasingly litigious, led by the Americans. As a result, most competitors incorporate to limit personal liability, firms are allowed to advertise for the first time. The US economy goes into recession for 4 years, and EEC growth slows to less than 2 per cent a year. A shake-out in the profession is likely, with mergers and takeovers becoming more common; only large firms can cope with the size of investment in hardware, software and staff training required to service large clients.

This stage of the planning process is an integral part of the SWOT (strengths, weaknesses, opportunities, threats) analysis.

WHO ARE WE?

This may seem a strange question, but it is just as important for a service organisation as for a manufacturer to have a coherent and clear identity. When there are a number of dynamic professionals in a firm, each with his or her own patch, this may be difficult to achieve. One possibility is to plan for each business area separately, but a collection of disparate identities is likely to be much less powerful than one which, while broad, is mutually supportive and consistent.

The identity must reflect the people at the top – their values, skills, personalities. The view taken must be *objective*, and it is this need for objectivity that has led to firms employing outside consultants when starting on the planning process. It is given to few to be truly objective about themselves, but it is an absolutely essential starting point (see Chapter 5 – Analysing Strengths and Weaknesses).

WHO DO WE WANT TO BE?

The answer to this may of course be 'The same as we are now'. This is a perfectly acceptable position, provided that it can be sustained in the changing competitive world. For the energetic and ambitious professional, some development is likely to be built in to the view of the firm's future.

The Saatchi brothers had a clear vision of their identity at each stage of development, until perhaps it became too diffused. Equally, a small creative boutique can have a precise view of what it is and therefore what it can and cannot do. For a people-based organisation this question is fundamental

Creating the business plan

and must be argued out with great clarity. Probably the most common cause of the break-up of partnerships is disagreement as to future goals and directions. It is all too easy to assume that partners know and agree with each other's views. Of course individuals change: some want to go on conquering new worlds while others are happy with what they have. This only underlines the need to make these views clear to everyone concerned.

The future goal must refer back to the current position, and – human nature being what it is – the aspiration should be:

- *realistic*: attainable without too many miracles or transformations
- *stretching*: giving people something to aim at which will stretch them beyond their existing levels of achievement.

As so often, these should refer back to previous analyses. Great leaders such as Alexander the Great or Dame Ninette de Valois could make people perform beyond what they as individuals would have considered possible. If the firm has such inspirational leaders, it can set very demanding targets; otherwise ambition must be tempered with realism.

Based on its judgement of possibilities, the firm must decide if it wants to be a leader or a follower, brilliant or sound, broad or specialist, high-tech or people-oriented. Some of these aspects of culture may seem vague, but they do affect how the firm is seen by current and prospective clients, and by current and prospective employees. Perceived culture may affect recruitment, motivation, dress and manners, office décor; it may also affect *results*, as Peters and Waterman suggested.[1]

Culture may be a powerful negative influence as well as a positive one, and is difficult to change. It is formed particularly by the people at the top, but is based also on history. Though difficult to quantify, it must be taken into account in planning.

WHERE ARE WE AND WHERE DO WE WANT TO BE?

These are parallel questions to the previous ones, and the answers should largely flow from the market and SWOT analyses described in the previous two chapters.

Resulting from all these should be a *mission statement* encapsulating the firm's view of itself, its strengths and weaknesses, its product–market scope and its aspirations. The statement must be general, so that it is not out of date in a year or two, but specific enough to guide choices and actions. It should avoid pious hopes and pie-in-the-sky.

From the mission statement, the diagnosis of resources and the view of the future currently held, should come a set of objectives. Objectives should if possible be quantified rather than vague: '15 per cent market share in 3 years' rather than 'large', or 'growth in sales of 10 per cent per year' rather than 'fast-growing'.

The purpose of setting objectives is to help form action plans, and to give performance standards so that achievement can be checked against aspiration. Without specific objectives it is difficult to decide priorities, or to measure whether or not performance is up to expectations. As the old saying has it, 'If you don't know where you're going, any road will do.'

Objectives can be usefully stated for the following areas:

Financial	Total sales
	Total profit
	Profit on sales
	Return on investment, capital employed, equity, etc.
	Assets growth
	Debt/equity ratio
	Creditor and debtor periods
	Cost ratios (staff, admin., etc.)
Marketing	Total sales
	Market share, total and by segment
	New markets to be tackled
	New products to be developed
Operations (to be defined as appropriate)	Bids accepted as percentage of tenders
	Percentage of reports on time
	Number of complaints
	Satisfaction ratings
General	To go public in 4 years
	Satisfy personal partnership ambitions
	Accommodate other socio-economic factors

Creating the business plan

HOW SHALL WE GET THERE?

Only after all the careful diagnosis and forecasting set out above has been carried out can any operational planning begin. Armed with the analysis of where we are now, the mission statement and objectives, the firm can take a broad-brush view of the next 5 years. (Five is not a sacred number, but has been found a workable period by many people; 3 is probably a minimum to allow any reasonable lead time, and beyond 5 years the uncertainty becomes so large as to swamp the usefulness of planning.) This is equivalent to planning in outline how to get to a destination for a holiday in Spain: 'by car, taking the Dover–Calais ferry, staying off motorways wherever possible, passing west of Paris, taking two overnight stops . . .'

An important part of this stage is the generation and evaluation of options. It is easy to project current methods forward as if they were the only ones available. There is sense in this, as we ought at least to know what we are doing if we use well-tried ways. At the planning stage, however, we can and must look at other possibilities; we can after all do so without risk. Sometimes the objectives set *force* a firm to look for innovative ways of doing business, either because current methods will not produce the required growth or because substantial cost savings are necessary.

Creativity is often needed to get away from the tunnel vision that restricts most people's view of the future. It is sometimes thought that only certain people are creative, while others are not. The evidence does not bear this out: most people can be creative if they allow themselves to be and if the situation encourages it. This is the thinking behind such techniques as brainstorming. A group is given a problem, and a limited time to produce as many solutions as possible. No evaluation (cries of 'Rubbish' or 'That's impossible' from participants) is allowed, and *all* ideas are recorded. Brainstorming can be carried out by individuals on their own, and some argue that this is more productive.

Evaluation should be seen as a separate stage from the generation of ideas, and here rigour and logic come into their own. Each option must be evaluated objectively, no matter who its author is (though this can be personally or politically sensitive).

This process of examining broad outlines is important because it allows a check on the feasibility of getting from where we are to where we want to be in 5 years. Are there any huge jumps? What resources will be needed? What might stop us? What contingency plans will we need to deal with drastic changes in conditions?

A useful way of looking at the 5-year progress is to separate growth from existing business and that to be obtained from new business. This is dealt with in detail in Chapters 2 and 7, on market analysis and strategic marketing planning, but its importance cannot be over-stressed here. Again, it is a check on the feasibility of the plan and the nature and scale of the task ahead.

DETAILED PLANNING

There should be a detailed plan for 1 year: it should specify detailed objectives and spell out programmes to achieve them, identifying what actions need to be taken by whom and when. If the business is a broad one, containing several distinct parts, the detailed planning should be done separately for each.

Starting from the mission statement and long-range objectives, the plan should contain the following sections:

1 *Situation analysis* Summarising the SWOT analysis, competitive situation and market forecasts.

2 *Objectives* Detailed objectives for the year in terms of results (sales, profitability, profits, market share, new developments).

3 *Marketing* Target segments, detailed programmes.

4 *Financial* Two sets of plans – cash flow and finance. The cash flow plan for the year is vitally important; it reflects the marketing plan, informs the financial plan, and forecasts how much cash will be needed when. The financial plan sets out how the necessary finance will be provided and sets targets for key ratios.

5 *Operations* For a service organisation these relate mainly to staff. If the firm bills on a time-fee basis, the sales targets need to be translated into staff days, separating out days spent selling, administering, managing and actually carrying out the substantive work. Apart from feeding back to the financial and marketing plans, these calculations lead to planning for *recruitment* and *training*. Support staff also need to be brought into the plan.

6 *Premises and equipment* Unplanned growth can lead to chaos in working conditions. For some firms, reliance on information technology means that this section of the plan will assume great importance, as breakdown here can effectively stop the organisation delivering its service.

REVIEW AND CONTROL

However good the plan, it must be kept under review. There is no point spending a great deal of expensive and scarce management time producing a plan only to put it in a drawer and ignore it. Indeed, to leave out a feedback and control mechanism is to cease to plan at all. Consider the function of a thermostat in a central heating system: by monitoring results against the targets set, it controls the operation of the system by switching the boiler on and off. Without the thermostat, the system would be out of control; similarly with a company plan.

Operation of the 1-year plan needs to be reviewed regularly and frequently, probably at least every 3 months. Weekly or monthly targets will of course be reviewed at departmental level, but the whole plan should be reviewed by top management in a rigorous and objective way throughout the year.

The 5-year plan also needs to be reviewed and revised in the light of experience and changing conditions. This will happen naturally every year, but it may be that a fundamental reassessment is scheduled every 2 or 3 years.

EXAMPLE BUSINESS PLAN

EXECUTIVE EDUCATORS LTD
Business Plan, 1988

(Note: this plan is based on a real example, disguised to prevent identification.)

Mission statement

Executive Educators Ltd (EEL) will offer, through a team of the best management teachers available in Europe, high-quality in-house programmes tailored to the needs of large companies and other organisations. The service offered will be seen by clients as a vital part of the implementation of their corporate strategy; the programmes will start at board level and cascade down through middle management. EEL will be seen as the leader in its field in the UK by 1995.

Objectives

1. To go public via the USM in 1995, thereby rewarding founders and major participants with substantial capital gains.
2. To increase the value of shares tenfold by the time of the public launch.
3. To reach a before-tax profit of £1 million by 1995.
4. To generate sufficient cash during years 3 to 7 to buy a teaching facility in London and one or more residential properties in the country.
5. To achieve the above through long-term relationships with a small number of large clients.
6. To create a reward system which will attract and keep very high quality teaching staff.

Environment and market assessment

In the late 1980s management education and training have become a hot topic. The publication of the national reports by Handy[2] and by Constable and McCormick,[3] followed by the setting-up of the Management Charter Initiative, have ensured that, in large companies at least, management development is very much on the agenda. The reports quoted recommended a massive expansion of provision, but also pointed out that the current infrastructure in universities and polytechnics would be quite unable to meet this demand.

Although hard figures for market size are not available, it is clear that growth is substantial. All the leading providers report full order books and waiting lists.

It is felt that this situation will not change dramatically over the next 5 years at least, since international competition is increasing, and British firms are aware that they will have to fight hard to survive. Highly trained managers will be a vital part of the competitive armoury.

The demand will therefore continue to grow at 15 to 30 per cent per year. The share of total market needed by EEL to reach its targets is small, and attainable.

Competition

The main competitors are university business schools in UK and Europe, such as London and Manchester Business Schools, INSEAD, IMEDE, Cranfield; private institutions such as Ashridge; and possibly UK and American private companies.

In terms of strength and weaknesses, the university business schools have good reputations in some areas, but are seen as too theoretical and removed from practice. They also treat management education as peripheral to their main concerns. Their capacity is limited, and already stretched.

The private providers are potentially threatening, but the growth of the market should mean that there is plenty of business for all. New competition will be limited by the supply of top-quality teachers.

Positioning of EEL

EEL will be as intellectually rigorous as the universities, but essentially practical and in tune with business. Its teachers will be the best in their field in terms of knowledge *and* ability to teach managers. At the head will be 'stars', but they will be backed up by a strong team of competent lower-level professionals.

It will offer a dedicated, flexible service to clients on a long-term basis. Courses can be offered on clients' premises, or in hotels or purpose-designed training facilities.

A key concept is *partnership* with clients in the design and delivery of programmes. Other key words in the EEL promise are that it will be *businesslike* and *professional*.

Premises and equipment

Premises initially were rented from an associate company, with a move to its own office suite late in the first year. The plan is for a move to larger premises in year 2 or 3, with the acquisition of specialist teaching facilities a further year later. Residential 'country house' property will be bought in years 4 and 5, depending on cash flow.

Initial equipment included normal office equipment, plus Apple Mac II computers with laser printer. The plan envisages purchase of further Apples as the staff expands. Cash-flow forecasts include these, with networking and up-to-date communications. All support the quality of what is delivered.

Staffing

The operation started with two full-time directors, one full-time secretary and one temp. During year 1 a full-time administrator joined, together with six associate consultants.

During year 2 a further full-time principal and two support staff will be recruited. Depending on sales, one or more junior professionals will also start. In subsequent years all categories of staff will continue to build up in parallel to sales growth. The recruitment and training of good young staff who can be brought up to the level needed is an integral part of the plan, since the supply of competent senior staff will be insufficient.

A key feature of the recruitment package is the offer of shares and share options to attract the best teachers. Salaries will be competitive with the best going market rate, with bonuses for outstanding performance; cars are provided for all senior staff. The total package is therefore much better than available in business schools.

Marketing

Target markets   Primary targets are identified as:
- Large companies and other organisations which are either undergoing some major challenge (new competition, restructuring, increased growth targets), or are in the process of implementing a strategy calling for improved managerial performance.
- Early adopters are those within the total segment whose top management see the development of their human resources as a vital part of strategic implementation. Those signing on for the Management Charter Initiative are obvious targets, as are those who already send large numbers of managers on courses.
- Sectors seen as priority include banks, such other financial services as building societies, professional service firms, large retailers, newly privatised corporations.

Decision-makers need to be identified within target companies. They will include managing director, personnel director and training manager as gatekeeper and recommender. Specific messages will be targeted at each.

Promotion is through high-quality printed material (corporate brochure and course leaflets) and direct selling by senior staff. Direct mail will be used to find leads other than those brought in by the personal contacts of directors and associates. Prime targets will receive some material every 3 months to remind them of EEL's existence and services. This material will include information on new courses, and any relevant items such as publications by staff, major contracts gained, etc. The existing data base will become increasingly sophisticated over time, allowing precise targeting of messages. Media advertising will be used only sparingly.

Finance

Initial capital is authorised at 1 million shares, the majority still unissued to allow sales and options to new principals and staff.

Equipment is funded by long-term loans, with a bank overdraft facility for working capital. Cash-flow forecasts suggest that this is sufficient, but a small proportion of shares could be sold to investors if liquidity becomes a problem. This would be in any case a short-term difficulty only, as the nature of the business means that it generates large amounts of cash.

Control and review

The board reviews the results against plan every 3 months, making adjustments where necessary.

[Note: in practice, substantial adjustments were necessary, owing to personnel changes and a longer than forecast lead time for some sales.]

Detailed forecasts

[There followed very detailed spreadsheets forecasting cash flow and profit and loss for 5 years, with outline figures for a further 2. These are not reproduced here as they would not be informative. They must, of course, be carried out by anyone trying to plan seriously. Spreadsheets make the job very much easier, but the rule remains, 'Garbage in, garbage out'. The assumptions behind forecasts must be stated and examined carefully, particularly if the figures look very optimistic. Spreadsheets allow rapid recalculation of quite complex sets of figures, and can be used to test results for sensitivity.]

REFERENCES

1   Peters, T.J., and Waterman, R.H.,   *In Search of Excellence* (Harper & Row, 1982)

2   Handy, C., *The Making of Managers* (NEDO, April 1987)

3   Constable, J., and McCormick, R., *The Making of British Managers* (BIM/CBI, 1987)

7

STRATEGIC MARKETING PLANNING

by Michael Brewer

EDITOR'S PREVIEW

Michael Brewer is a marketing consultant with Marketing Solutions Ltd. His consultancy experience includes several projects with the Training Agency (formerly the Manpower Services Commission) on the development of open learning and the promotion of adult training to British industry. He has also worked on projects for government departments and the financial services sector.

A good strategic plan should evoke ACTION – not just be a passive document. That is the key message from Michael Brewer in this chapter on strategic planning. Experience can only be acquired as a result of taking action and observing the effect of that action. The fear of getting it wrong must be no excuse for inaction. After all, the whole purpose of business and strategic planning is to minimise the risk of getting it wrong.

Peter Drucker writes: 'The best plan is *only* good intentions unless it leads *into work*.'[1] The marketing plan which you develop is useless if it does not consist of actions as well as ideas, and timescales as well as objectives. Its place should be on your desk, among working papers, not on the shelf with reference books (like this one!).

Drucker also describes planning as 'the application of thought, analysis, imagination and judgement. It is responsibility, rather than technique.'[2] There are no magic formulas or foolproof forms to fill in which will deliver a perfectly shaped marketing plan into your hands.

Like babies, plans require the commitment, collaboration and co-operation of you and your partners; and, like children, they benefit over time with an input of knowledge and the feedback of experience.

PREPARATION

Before starting on the marketing plan you should have completed the Business Plan which contains a statement of the company aims and objectives (see Chapter 6). A clear view of the key activities and financial conditions is an essential part of the framework for the marketing plan.

An understanding of the market-place, your target customers and competitors is the other part of the framework (see chapter 4). These are the key external factors affecting the plan, as shown in Figure 7.1.

INTERNAL FACTORS	EXTERNAL
– Objectives	– Target customers
– Finance	– Competitors

FIGURE 7.1 Marketing strategy/plan

THE PLANNING PROCESS

As the marketing plan is developed, the assumptions which underline objectives and financial constraints will be tested. Are they consistent? Is the target market large enough – or too broadly defined? Can a workable plan which matches or beats the competition be created? Do we actually know enough to answer these questions – or is more research necessary?

Imaginative, creative thinking will be required to answer some of these questions. Few people are naturally creative in a way which will enable them to produce an imaginative and effective plan. This is why a collaborative approach by several partners or managers will produce the best plan, even if one person has responsibility for producing the final, written version.

Input from others can be made in several ways: circulating a draft for comment, for example, or asking individuals to look at specific areas or issues on which they have strong opinions, or relevant experience. Alternatively brainstorming sessions can be set up to review options or thrash out ideas. This approach is particularly useful as a means of building support for the plan. Success, however, depends on careful management of the session. Ideally, briefing notes should be sent round beforehand, and a structured agenda used for the meeting. A time limit should be set (2–3 hours at most), and any source of interruption (e.g. telephone calls) prevented or avoided as far as possible.

Once produced, the plan should be reviewed regularly, and you may find it effective to follow the same approach for reviews as was used in originating the plan.

Finally the plan should always be written/typed. This may seem obvious, yet many small business managers believe they know what they are going to do, and that they will be able to remember later why they did it. Time spent on writing plans, which may well soon change, can be better spent on real business, they feel. This temptation must be resisted. A written plan is as vital a record of progress and activity in marketing as keeping the books is for financial management.

STRUCTURE OF THE STRATEGY AND PLAN

The format used in this section follows the four Ps described in Chapter 1.

- Product
- Price
- Place
- Promotion

Experience has shown that these four headings cover all aspects of the marketing function, providing you interpret them carefully to reflect the type of company and market-place. The purpose of the following section is to help you to make that interpretation, so that you can develop a plan which reflects the particular characteristics of your business.

SETTING OBJECTIVES

Commercial objectives

Start the plan with a statement of the commercial objectives you wish, or intend, to achieve. These targets will form the basis for the calculations to be made on sales, promotional budgets, pricing and discounting, etc.

The key headings are:

- Sales value
- Profit

For the purposes of the marketing strategy and plan, relate the financial objectives to the target customers and products of the business:

1. How much revenue will come from each type of customer or market sector? For architects, say, how much from local authorities compared to public companies? For solicitors, say, how much, from each local office?

2. What will the sales mix be? Which products or services will be most significant to the business, and in what proportions? The answer may be relatively simple (in an estate agency, for example) or more complex. It may be unpredictable at the start for a new business; an existing business can look back and make decisions on changing the sales mix.

In most cases the timescale suitable for these objectives can be split between 1 year and 3 to 5 years. The difference is in what you intend to focus on and achieve in the immediate future, compared to what you want to establish eventually.

There may also be long-term threats or opportunities for which you should allow or even be prepared. For example, several parts of the service sector are influenced by political and legal systems. Changes in law relating to finance, legal services, health care, property, buildings, may all be expected in the UK, not least as a result of the impending 'Europeanisation' in 1992.

Marketing objectives

There is a range of marketing objectives which may be included in the plan. Growth, changing position in the market, resisting a threatening move from a competitor, all demand decisive actions:

- Entering new market sectors/reaching new customers; whether by region/area or of a different type, e.g. adding corporate business to private; or opening new local offices.
- Extending the product/service range, e.g. providing automobile insurance to existing domestic insurance customers.
- Raising prices/changing the price structure, e.g. from fixed fees to variable costs, or from a single charge to a variable, composite charge.
- Changing the image or identity of the business among existing or new customers, either as a result of or in association with objectives like those above, or as an exercise in itself to reach a new position in the market, e.g. as an exclusive, high-quality service rather than a general-purpose agency, or as a specialist rather than an all-rounder.

Each of these objectives represents a fundamental change for the company. Each may or will have significant implications for the costs and revenue of the business.

The purpose of this section is not to state, or decide, how these objectives will be achieved. Rather, it is to state how the managers of the business believe it will meet the needs of its customers, while resisting or responding to the environmental and market-place pressures.

Making objectives achievable

Responding to the market-place does not imply that you must simply wait around to see what happens in the market and then react. That course of action will ensure that at most you are number 2 (if you have the best market intelligence, and the fastest decision-making), and at worst out of business.

Remember the Sony Walkman. Its makers did not respond to a specific need, but created a product which allowed people to do something new and enjoyable. In other words, they led the market by understanding the interests and preferences which people have in listening to music.

Marketing objectives will be achievable in the broad sense if they come from an in-depth understanding of the customer, and the reasons for choosing the product. For your business they must also relate to your commercial objectives and the resources available to fund activity.

Past experience, or the track record of competitors, teaches what has been achieved under particular conditions. If those conditions have altered – and deregulation in finance markets is a classic case – new opportunities and threats will appear. Take them into account and do not try to repeat the past. Equally, do not expect to defy past experience without high risk. Achievable objectives seek to improve on the past, maintaining good performance in difficult conditions, increasing it in favourable conditions.

PRODUCT DEFINITION AND SALES PLANNING

Product features and benefits

A product description should be expressed in terms of its *features* and the corresponding *benefits* for the customer.

Features

What does your product consist of? The answer to this question has implications for cost as well as sales. The more features you build into a product, the higher the cost may become – and the higher the price to the customer.

Defining the product in a service company can be a complex exercise, since there may be features which do not at first appear to be part of the product. The customers may not consciously consider them as features, and yet will still alter their buying behaviour as a result of their absence or presence.

The various methods used to present services are an example. Is your office part of the product? Are plans, certificates or other documents part of the product? The answer is often 'yes', as the customers feel they are not receiving value for money, or begin to question the quality of a service, because it is badly presented. Conversely, attractive offices and efficient paperwork build confidence and repeat business.

Other features of the product in a service business include the way enquiries are handled (e.g. by receptionists), speed of response to briefs, and use of special equipment or resources which may affect the service. For example, an estate agent might add the services of a surveyor to the basic product of house sale/purchase.

Benefits

The features describe what your business is going to do; each one should translate into a benefit which is perceived by the customers as something of value when they make a purchase. If the dentist sells toothbrushes at a higher price than local shops, there is little benefit to the customer. If he sells specialist toothbrushes which are unobtainable locally, then the customer benefits. The dentist with many business people as customers could install a pay telephone or even a free telephone – to let them stay in touch with their offices. The 'feature' of a telephone translates into a practical benefit.

Product positioning and branding

When defining the product, it is as well to keep in mind what your competitors are doing. Are any of them offering any special features? Or are they all doing exactly the same thing? To be totally different from your competitors, in a market where the majority of players are similar, may confuse your customers of course. However, where a point of difference which makes your product stand out can be established, you can benefit by attracting the customers' attention and providing additional reasons to buy from you.

Finally, it may be possible to brand or package the products. Grouping similar products under one name, offering them as a 'package' – like the estate agent who also provides a surveying service, or the building society which organises a solicitor – creates a distinctive product which can be given a label or brand name. The name can help to explain the product to target customers, or simply be more memorable than a straightforward description. Brand names can also differentiate a product from similar or identical competitive products.

Starting the sales plan

The sales plan is developed from a balance between market conditions and productive capacity in the firm.

Bear in mind that many markets are seasonal. Consumers demand less of some services during the summer holiday season than during autumn and winter – and vice-versa. Demand may vary by time of week, or time of day. Businesses respond to these variations, as well as to the timing of their budget systems and financial years. Local authorities and government departments often spend more, or are more open to discuss purchases, at the end of a financial year (the spring), or during planning for the next year (summer/autumn), than at other times.

As for productive capacity, internal resources dictate the sales with which you can reasonably expect to cope. In many service businesses this capacity may be the total of number of people multiplied by the hours they are prepared to work. Any increase in sales requires an increase in head count.

Where sales are not directly related to hours, the total potential capacity should still be calculated. How many projects can be handled? How many customers serviced? What are the upper limits on sales which can be managed, taking into account holidays, equipment or other facilities which must be used, etc.?

Combining the information on market conditions and internal capacity will produce a set of sales targets in terms of 'volume' of product sold. For Year 1, these targets should be broken down by month or even week, so that variations in demand/supply can be adequately reflected. For Years 2 and 3, the sales targets can be quarterly or half-yearly, as predictions will be more difficult to make, and resources do not need to be planned in such detail.

PRICE SETTING AND SALES PLANNING

By now you will be well aware that marketing planning is a balance between the needs of the customer and the capability of the business. Nowhere is this balance more sensitive and urgent than in setting prices for products.

Cost plus

Careful calculation of costs in offering the product for sale is essential for financial health. In certain cases – usually when you are in a commodity market, or a monopoly – prices to the consumer can be set on a cost-plus basis. Either they dictate to you how much margin you can take, or you dictate to them how much they will have to pay.

Some service markets may also be limited by regulations, either imposed or agreed, which define the price to the customer. However, even if such conditions apply, it is still valuable to look at pricing in the light of customer views.

The customer viewpoint

Successful products are priced to reflect the value customers believe they receive, at least in economic terms. Analysis of customers' reactions is an important indicator of how price levels can be set and the possible benefits of increases or decreases to the business.

Customers do not act entirely rationally in making purchase decisions of course, particularly when purchasing service products which are difficult to evaluate. We never know for certain whether a different doctor, solicitor or bank manager would have done a better job for us. Building confidence in the customer's mind is essential, through efficiency of service and quality of presentation as well as quality of the product itself. Customers are prepared to pay more for a product which has 'added value' of this kind by comparison with competitors.

Similarly, customers may judge the quality of a product by its costs. A capitalist world generates few genuine high-quality low-cost products, especially in service businesses. If you want your high-quality product to be perceived as such, do not price it at the level of the ordinary product –

unless you have an exceptional cost advantage and can afford to spend money explaining to the customer what you are doing.

The competitive situation

Your customers will almost certainly judge the value of your product by comparison with your competitors. The third starting point for pricing therefore is what your competitors charge. If you are offering the same product, and can afford to charge less, you will win their customers – at least until they cut their prices, perhaps below yours.

A better strategy is to match your competitors' price if the product offering is similar; or better still, to vary the product and charge on a different basis.

Pricing a product range

Selling a range of products can provide an opportunity to follow different principles with different items. One might be offered at a cost-plus price or even free, to attract customers, e.g. the free or low-price estimate for a project (the price of which should include the cost of producing the estimate). High prices might be charged on products or services which are peripheral to the core business but attractive to certain customers who do not wish to go elsewhere.

Sales planning

The impact of price on sales volume has already been mentioned. In the market-place it is an effect which cannot always be measured, although experience of the market or specific tests help to make judgements easier.

For the business, price levels and the sales volume targets should be combined to produce the sales revenue plan. A personal computer spreadsheet programme is an eminently suitable tool for this exercise. When the data has been fed in, variations in costs, sales and prices can be tested to assess the implications for the business.

One of the most interesting and important calculations which can be made is in reviewing sales-mix changes. What happens if 50 per cent of our sales are product A, with a 35 per cent margin, rather than product B, with a 45 per cent margin? What would happen if an estate agent increased the average price of houses sold from £50,000 to £60,000 in a year, but sold 10 per cent fewer houses?

The results of sales-mix fluctuations may be enormous or insignificant, but exploring them in detail will allow you to see where the sensitivities of the business are. You may then exploit them, or protect yourself from problems, by attaching the right level of priority.

PLANNING FOR PLACE

The third of the four marketing Ps can be applied to service businesses of all types and sizes.

Management of premises

This aspect has already been discussed under the heading of product definition. If customers visit your premises, especially if the business is in a High Street location intended to attract customers, the style and quality of the building, rooms and facilities must be high enough to match their standards and expectations.

Location of premises

The relevance of geographical location depends on the nature and size of the business.

We can distinguish simply between retail and non-retail service businesses. Retail service businesses are largely consumer-orientated and include estate agents, banks, building societies, doctors, dentists – all those where the service is delivered on a site which must be accessible to the customer.

The guiding rule for such businesses is to identify where their target customers are concentrated, and where direct competitors are not well established. A small business seeking to expand locally can carry out the research directly, using local knowledge. A larger concern, seeking regional or national expansion, will use commercial data bases.

Non-retail service businesses are those where location is of less or no relevance to the customer – generally those where the target market is commercial or institutional, but including those where the contact with the consumer is by post or telephone (in the insurance sector, for example). For such businesses decisions on location can be directed by cost considerations, convenience for staff or opportunity.

Selection of distribution channels

You may decide that you want to reach new customers through others' premises, in addition to your own. The choice of distribution channels is very much a marketing decision, since the choice must be driven by the location and buying habits of the customer. That is not to say that you cannot change them – the High Street stockbroker shop is an attempt to do just that, though yet to be proven successful.

Distribution channel decisions may also offer you a means of differentiating the business from the competition, and reaching customers who would not normally be aware of, or have access to, your product and service. Any new step of this kind should of course be carefully researched and tested before a full launch.

PLANNING FOR PROMOTION

The term promotion is used here to cover all those activities designed to publicise your business and generate sales – advertising, direct mail, public relations, exhibitions, production and distribution of leaflets, posters, etc. A more detailed review of the options available and how to manage them is presented in Chapter 8.

Planning principles

Promotion is no more or less important in the marketing plan than product, price or the management of place. But because management of

Strategic marketing planning

the activity generally occupies so much more time during the year, planning promotion can receive more attention. Strong feelings are aroused by views on whether advertising degrades a prestigious business, or on the relative merits of one medium versus another.

In reply to these points we can confidently state that all methods of promotion are neutral and that it is how you use them that creates an image. The value of each method varies in respect of the number and type of people reached; the value to your business depends entirely on who you want to reach, and with what message. You will only know the answer if you measure and evaluate all the activity you undertake.

Research has shown that when people make a decision to buy, they have usually gone through a process which can be summed up under four headings:

1 *Awareness* When they first learn of the product or service, from other people, advertising or other promotion.

2 *Interest* Once aware, their interest is caught, probably because they realise the benefit which the product offers to them, and they try to find out more.

3 *Desire* The interest is or becomes strong enough to make them consider seriously whether they should follow up the interest.

4 *Action* Desire becomes action when a purchase is made, although the action may also be to ask for more information in order to make a decision.

Think back to the time you bought a new product from the supermarket, and you will be able to see how you went through these stages.

A television advertisement, a poster or perhaps a friend made you aware of the product first. You were interested and looked for it, or asked about it. When you found it, you decided it was what you wanted, and you made the purchase.

In planning promotions, you can make use of the framework. Remember, though, that if you are in the services market, the 'Action' people take may well be to ask for more information – such as an estimate of costs – before purchasing.

Setting objectives for promotion

Awareness and action are the starting points for your promotional objectives.

Awareness-building should be designed to make sure that your company and product are as well known as possible among potential customers. This aim is always important, but can be expensive, and hard to justify if you are one of many competing businesses – just because they know about you doesn't mean they will choose you. On the other hand, if you have few competitors, awareness may be all you need to bring customers to your door.

Advertising – on television, radio, posters, or in magazines or papers – is the most common method of building awareness, because it reaches so many people so quickly. Press or public relations (PR) is another way, one which is cheaper but less reliable.

An action-generating promotion is focused on selling your products by telling potential customers what the benefits are, where they can buy the product from you, how much it costs, and so on. Advertising can be used for this purpose, but can be an expensive method. Specialist magazine advertising – trade papers or hobby papers, for example – is usually best because it is directed towards people with specific interests. Other methods are direct mail, exhibition stands, and door-to-door leaflet drops.

Action-generating objectives are basically of two kinds:

- Selling more to existing customers.
- Attracting new customers.

Common sense says that it is often easier to sell more to existing customers, for they know you and trust you (if service has been good!). How you sell more will depend on whether your customers need more of the same product or not. You may want to add new products – like building societies that offer conveyancing or banks that give mortgages.

If there is nothing more to sell to existing customers, then you may aim to attract new customers – from another area or in another sector, or from the same base as your existing customers if you are confident that there are many more you are not reaching and that your competitors are not much stronger than you. As a rule of thumb, your chances of success are greatest if you start with existing customers and existing products (see Figure 7.2).

Strategic marketing planning

OPTIONS	EXISTING PRODUCT	NEW PRODUCT
EXISTING MARKET	1	3
NEW MARKET	2	4

FIGURE 7.2 Options

Get the most from these before you start to move on to new products and markets.

Your objectives could be something like the following:

- to increase awareness of our company among purchasing managers in food companies
- to increase the sales of the Chichester office
- to promote the new product we are launching in September.

Setting a budget for promotion

Deciding how much you will spend on promotions is one of the most difficult marketing questions. There are no simple formulas!

Your promotional budget should be affordable of course. One must look at the percentage of sales or gross profit which could reasonably be allocated. It is unwise to anticipate sales increases as a result of promotional activity.

Then compare what you could afford with the pattern of your business. If people take action as a result of the promotion, what will be the value of the average transaction? An architectural practice might be aiming for a contract worth several hundred thousand pounds, with a mark-up of 100 per cent. A dentist might expect an average spend per customer of £50 per year.

The questions you must then ask are:

1 How many additional sales are required to justify this promotional spend?

2 What proportion of our existing business is that? Have we the resources to cope?

3 What proportion of the total market does that represent? Can we realistically expect to reach all those people and persuade them?

The answers to these questions will help you to develop a sense of proportion. The possible budget can be adjusted to reflect a reasonable balance of cost vs result.

Allocating the budget

The last question listed above leads into the issue of effectiveness. How much can you expect to achieve by different promotional methods? Which should we choose to get the most from our money?

A more detailed review of communication options is contained in Chapter 8. At this point the key factors are that effectiveness increases in relation to

- the accuracy of targeting
- the opportunity for action.

Accurate targeting is easiest with

- direct mail, if you have an up-to-date list of postential customers
- exhibitions (for your area or sector)
- retail locations (near customers).

Opportunities for action are greatest when

- the mailshot aids response (order forms; pre-printed envelopes)
- orders can be taken or sales made at the exhibition
- advertisements include coupons, telephone numbers or addresses
- retail locations display products/services attractively.

The type of product you offer must also influence the allocation. Does it need to be seen or demonstrated to be appreciated? Does it need to be explained carefully to be understood? If so, some element of personal contact may be necessary, and advertising will probably be ineffective for generating action.

You will be well advised when you make the allocation to select a relatively small number of activities. The more you attempt to do, the greater the chance of diluting management effort and resources, your message, and the result achieved. Keep it simple and high-quality, and you will meet the needs of the vast majority of your target customers.

REFERENCES

1 Drucker, Peter, *Management: Tasks, Responsibilities, Practices* (Heinemann, 1974)

2 *Ibid.*

8

A REVIEW OF THE COMMUNICATIONS OPTIONS
by Norman Allen

EDITORS' PREVIEW

Norman Allen is managing director of Allen Fletcher Interact Ltd, a London-based agency with experience in a number of specialist business-to-business markets.

In this chapter Norman Allen summarises all the media channels that are available and demonstrates the importance of the 'creative' element. Consistency of message exposure is also stressed, and is summed up in the last sentence of the chapter: 'Familiarity may breed contempt, but it also breeds total recall.'

FIRST PRINCIPLES

The communications channels that are available within the mainstream of advertising and publicity are prodigious. In a broad market-based communications plan there are a large number of communications tools which meet specific needs and answer certain requirements. Many of these tools are used collectively to produce a successful synergy.

It is the generally accepted rule that no *one* option can be expected to achieve results by itself, but rather needs the support of other media options to gain satisfactory impact. These communications options range from the simple implementation of a press release to a comprehensive PR plan, to direct mail, brochures, posters, press advertisements, right through to a full-blooded TV campaign.

In any business, as well as the professional services, a number of considerations need to be addressed before any sensible investment can be made:

- What level of expenditure per year can be afforded?
- Who are the potential customers?
- Where and how can they best be reached?
- What strategy will be best to communicate with the market effectively?

There are many fundamentally obvious but incorrect routes to take, and there are others that are less obvious. For example, it is unlikely that you would advertise bibles in the *Racing Gazette* or exhaust systems in *Photography*. Nor would you sell headache pills in the *Lancet*, or silk underwear in the *Law Society Gazette*. This is obvious enough, but just as many outrages occur because the problems aren't so obvious.

Consider the following:

- Would you sell retirement homes through cinema advertising?
- Would you offer legal advice on bus posters?
- Would an estate agent advertise on the London Underground?
- Would an interior designer make his point on local radio?
- Why shouldn't the local Tandoori house get more customers by advertising on litter-bin stickers?

Each of these and most other professional services have very specific markets to appeal to. And who is likely to agree a budget that has inaccurate market targeting or high readership wastage? The image of your profession must be considered, and how your integrity, quality of service, type of person you wish to appeal to, will be affected by the medium you use to communicate through.

The local builder would more effectively run simple advertisements in his local paper during down times, supplementing them with a simple mailing letter to households that are likely to be in the market for extension and renovation work. He would also scan the local council office announcements for recent planning applications in order to build a list of 'hot prospects'. The local car repair specialists would also use local press advertising, supplemented by a simple handbill inserted under the windscreen wipers of cars in the nearby rail or supermarket car-parks. Such businesses' budgets would not extend to much more than that, but more importantly would not necessarily need to, even if money was no barrier.

The following section will answer many questions on the use of options in communications, making it clear where money might be best invested.

THE AVAILABLE OPTIONS

National Television

The most powerful and most expensive media tool, it charges anything from £10,000 to £25,000 for a 40-second spot, plus production costs. It gives blanket audience coverage nationwide with bias to the low/middle income groups, and is suitable for high-volume consumer goods or nationwide services such as banking or insurance. Big companies may spend from £2 million to £8 million per annum.

Local TV

Time is allocated here through regional networks for more localised services – car dealerships, building societies and large estate agents. It caters for low-budget produced spots, and again broad audience coverage in the lower to middle income sector. A professional adviser would not rely on this alone, and therefore would need a budget of, say, £150,000 per annum in order to address other media functions.

Newspapers – National Dailies

Also a powerful medium, but expensive, with very broad audience coverage across the total socio-economic spectrum, the nationals vary from the quality broadsheets to the popular tabloids. Cost considerations apart, there is high wastage in terms of relevant readership.

Newspapers – Regional and Local

The local weeklies and free sheets are a good medium for local businesses and professional services, with high readers-per-copy ratio. Being weekly, your message stays around for a longer time than a daily, and the rates are very reasonable. Many local newspapers can offer a local mailing list by socio-economic grouping. Mailers can be brought in and delivered through local newsagents. A very reasonable and cost-effective package.

Radio – National

Similar to TV, but perhaps less powerful, national radio is, however, less expensive. It has a young audience profile, both male and female, but particularly young housewives.

Radio – Regional

Again having young profile, and broad socio-economic grouping, depending on region, regional radio is a good medium as support to press advertising, and very inexpensive in relation to impact; but don't forget production charges will rocket if you use well-known voice-over talent. It is perhaps not very suitable for more specialised professional services.

Posters

Considered largely as support media, posters could not be relied on alone. They usually support larger national advertising campaigns, press and TV, for products such as baked beans, beers, cigarettes and cars, especially on national billboard sites. They are very expensive in terms of space and print production. More localised poster sites can be found, mainly at railway stations. Again consider the audience and remember it is a *support medium*.

A review of the communications options

Press and public relations

PR is perhaps one of the most important and profitable communications routes for businesses in the early development stage, when there is a need to build credibility without the resources to embark upon an advertising campaign. PR is the only communications vehicle that can operate without support media, in that while it is always a key part of any major advertising plan, it can also operate effectively alone. PR can cater for all levels of need financially, from simple press releases and articles in local newspapers to a full public relations plan encompassing the whole of a company's image needs internally as well as externally – organising promotions, or generating news items.

Cinema

A very effective resource, whether as part of a larger national spend or for the promotion of more local services, cinema has a captive audience with a youthful (16–35) profile, and the advantage of a large-screen format. It is inexpensive in relation to impact, but production costs need to be carefully considered. It has proved an ideal medium for conveyancing (first-time home buyers), local restaurants, leisure centres, motor dealerships, local stores, etc.

Video

What a useful and inexpensive tool! It can often be produced in-house by a competent enthusiast. A low-cost medium, it has a total demonstration and story capability – a moving brochure in fact! However, limited production runs mean that it should be reserved for limited use and for prospects who are likely respondents.

Journal Advertising

A key communications tool for businesses where specialised or local publications exist, it comprises local industry and business magazines and county magazines (*Kent Life*, *Essex Business*, etc.). It has the advantage of a specific reader profile and interest, and colour or black and white advertising. (Colour rates are at least twice the price of a black and white, and can be much more.)

House Drops

Acorn has a very good listing nationwide of selected area targeting on a regional basis. A simple leaflet can be dropped into selected households virtually street by street, so that you can accurately determine the income bracket that you wish to cover. It is ideal for specific local services.

Others

Information may be disseminated through county shows, sports centres, squash and golf clubs, colleges of further education, or by sponsorship of local art and music events. These are useful low-cost promotional areas that can also engender a sense of commitment to the local community.

THE CREATIVE ELEMENT

Every communications option offers creative opportunities that can be exploited in order to enhance and intensify the visibility of your message, in words as well as pictures.

There is little point in investing in an effective means to target the audience if the message is badly presented or the strategy ill-structured. Costs for such services vary considerably, but any number exist to cover all budget levels – from the local PR and marketing agency to design studios and freelance artists. Whichever route you take, even if you do it yourself, each route has its own opportunity for greater effectiveness in communications through creative ingenuity.

A direct mail shot does not have to be just a piece of folded A4 card. Cut-out shapes can add interest. Self-erecting three-dimensional constructions can intrigue and may stay around longer before being consigned to the garbage bin than simple leaflets.

Advertisements that have short, intriguing headlines rather than a bland statement will focus reader attention on your message rather than elicit a yawn. A cinema film with colourful graphics and a good, clear-voiced announcer is not expensive. The presentation will add an air of authority or humour to the audience's perception of your business. A short evocative statement on a poster will make the audience remember your name, but do not use lengthy copy. It won't be read.

It is always worth remembering all the cost-effective miscellaneous options that offer creative imagination and can add to the general publicity mix. Badges and balloons, for example, may be given away at local events. Car stickers may help garages or insurance companies. Refuse-bin stickers may work well for a skip-hire company or a hardware store.

Cost-effectiveness

An exemplary instance of cost-effective advertising may find favour through the opportunity of sharing costs. A firm of conveyancing lawyers that regularly deals with a firm of estate agents, which in turn passes on clients to an insurance broker, could share a local press and cinema campaign (young audience), to attract the attention of first-time home buyers, thereby sharing the expense and reaping the collective benefits.

Another true-life example of a low-cost direct mail campaign comes from a firm of local wine importers which distributed a mail shot for a wine-tasting event depicting a simple chart of popular wines and their origin, plus a 'year chart' showing the 'good years' for a particular wine. The 'educational' mailer stayed around a long time. The investment proved to be of great value in the sale of cases of wine over quite a long period.

This chapter has addressed the total range of options open in the mainstream of events. However, it is hoped that by viewing these in the broader sense, the individual will at least have both an understanding of how such opportunities will apply, or best suit the needs of the professional service advertiser. It simply adds up to understanding the client profile you are wishing to address and then determining the best medium through which to reach it. Cost can only be justified against an educated assumption of the expected response. However, remember that no single advertising insertion will bring the world to your door overnight; it is rather a case of continuous 'drip feed' until the message firmly registers. If the service is right and fits the market need, you'll get customers.

Familiarity may breed contempt, but it also breeds total recall.

9

SELECTING SUITABLE EXTERNAL SUPPORT SERVICES
by David Farbey

EDITORS' PREVIEW

David Farbey is managing director of Kingscott Advertising, and is a former Chairman of the Publicity Club of London, and currently a governor of the College of Distributive Trades.

In this chapter he explores what are often regarded as the shark-infested waters inhabited by advertising, public relations and direct marketing agencies. The right fish is there in the water, but careful preparation is required if the angler is to catch the fish, rather than the fish catch the angler.

PREPARING FOR ACTION

We have so far outlined the need for and the value of marketing programmes, which can achieve substantial commercial benefits for virtually any scale of operation. The small business or professional consultancy can think in marketing terms just as much as the large national organisation.

Marketing is not a matter of size, scale or type of business. It is a matter of outlook – and of organisation. Organising for marketing and thinking in marketing terms are the two bases of a successful performance. However, a successful action programme demands not only a suitable internal structure and staff appointment but also the satisfactory use of a range of outside support services, as and when they are required.

Marketing in action means doing a wide variety of things. It is not just a matter of planning, but performing. An action plan is only as good as its implementation, and from the point of view of day-to-day activity the normal type of business or professional consultancy does not (and usually cannot) possess all the necessary facilities or services within itself. External help is inevitable. So in practice much marketing activity consists of identifying, briefing, guiding and controlling those external suppliers or helpers whose skills and particular expertise are essential to making the action programme a success.

The marketing executive becomes a kind of impresario, juggling the contributions of a multitude of performers. The first step is to understand what categories of professional support may be required.

Marketing is a varied and wide-ranging concept, no two particular marketing programmes are precisely alike, and each marketing action plan must use only those resources specifically tailored to its own needs. But, in very general terms, it is likely that the following activities could be covered by an average marketing programme over the course of time.

Advertising Agencies

Providers of specialist services for paid-for advertising, as follows:

- planning and buying media space
- writing and designing advertisements
- producing advertisements ready to print
- planning general publicity strategies.

Public Relations Consultancies

Such consultancies supply programmes of publicity, especially in editorial columns or through editorial relations, often as 'unpaid' editorial comment.

Designers and Art Studios

They produce designs and artwork for graphic needs, ranging from letterheads to corporate styling to the design of brochures and literature.

Printers

Producers and deliverers of printed materials, they are used when office copiers and other equipment are not sufficient.

Mailing Houses

Where mailings are required to outside addressees, and the scale of the mailing is too large to handle within the office, specialist mailing houses may have to be used.

A variety of other specialists

To answer specific requirements, these include marketing consultants, market research companies for market research, exhibition contractors or stand fitters for exhibitions, etc.

The individual media of publicity

While you may use advertising agencies or public relations consultancies as intermediaries, you may also wish to have a direct contact from time to time with those media of communication that may be of potential help to you:

- local or regional newspapers
- local or regional magazines
- local radio

- regional TV
- directories, such as trade directories or Yellow Pages
- other media which perhaps would be less relevant but which still could be feasible, e.g. cinema, posters or local transport advertising.

We shall be looking at these categories individually, but a general need is apparent. If many outside services are available and may be used, it is crucial to have a clear view of the criteria for selecting them and judging them. Outside suppliers should be approached in an organised and systematic way, after a close analysis of what the organisation needs. That is:

- what is the precise commercial requirement?
- what specific type of outside service is needed to supply this?

Some of the relevant points to look for are:

1 *Type of service provided.* What is the *specific* service? You may not just want a printer, but a particular type of printer, e.g. litho colour specialist, particularly geared to brochure work, etc., and happy to handle small runs.

2 *Experience.* Has the supplier experience relevant to your own need? Ask for a statement of experience and look for examples.

3 *Size.* How large is the supplier? Is its size compatible with your own? Size is a major factor. Like generally works best with like. For instance, it is improbable that a multi-million pound London advertising agency would be happy with a three-person law practice spending hundreds rather than thousands of pounds in the outer provinces. Find the size with which you are most comfortable.

4 *Proximity.* Where is the supplier located? Is this convenient? Very often, the nearer is the better.

5 *Flexibility.* Can the outside service adjust to doing *your* thing *your* way? Can it work fast enough? Meet all the deadlines? Provide everything you need in the way that you need it? Often a supplier's internal system can dominate the service it provides. Its computer control should not be your master.

6 *Depth of service.* How well equipped is the service to handle you? Are there enough staff to give you sufficient time? Do they have enough coverage so as to protect your work-flow against sickness, absence, holidays, etc.?

7 *Cost.* This is obviously a key criterion and a major concern. Cost control and value for money are primary necessities. It is vital to ensure that the external service charges at a reasonable rate, provides what you are paying for, and does not let extra costs mount up once the work is under way. With these criteria in mind, individual types of service can now be examined.

ADVERTISING AGENCIES

The marketing programme may very well lead to a programme of marketing communications. Advertising agencies provide the main specialist service for this. It is possible for organisations to carry out their own advertising requirements

- if the workload is moderate
- if there are available staff
- if the job to be done is relatively simple.

But on the whole most advertisers prefer to use a properly equipped advertising agency for three practical reasons: (1) an agency has the expertise, (2) using an agency saves bother and reduces overheads, and (3) most of what the agency does should not cost extra, but comes from commissions offered by the media.

Here it may be helpful to define an advertising agency. It is a specialist in the creation and placement of advertising, which is 'recognised' as a bona fide advertising agency by the various media trading associations and which is largely paid by discounts granted to it by those media.

How to find an advertising agency

There are over 600 advertising agencies in Britain, located in most towns of any size. It may be possible to obtain a recommendation from colleagues, friends, other local businesses, the local business association (e.g. Rotary or the chamber of commerce) or from the local traders' association. Otherwise, names and addresses may be found in directories or lists, such as Yellow Pages, or *Advertisers' Annual*. Details are given at the end of the chapter (p. 144).

Advice on advertising agencies may also be obtained from the advertisers' own trade body – *The Incorporated Society of British Advertisers* (ISBA). This exists to protect the position of advertisers and is most helpful.

For details of local advertising agencies or for those with specialist skills, advice may also be obtained from *The Institute of Practitioners in Advertising*, which represents advertising agencies. It may not necessarily suggest a particular agency, but usually provides a short list of suitable possibilities for advertisers to examine.

What advertising agencies offer

Some advertising agencies concentrate only on providing advertising. But others may offer the complete range of marketing communications services, thereby offering a 'one-stop shop', i.e. the ability to obtain the whole of the marketing communications programme under one roof, through one supplier. This is, on the one hand, easier, simpler and more convenient, but, on the other, may mean placing too much reliance on one limited service.

Advertising agencies can offer the following:

1 Planning and campaign development.

2 Media planning, media evaluation and media buying.

3 Monitoring the appearance of advertisements as ordered.

4 Writing, design and production of advertisements.

5 Procurement of all necessary artwork and photography, drawings and illustrations, typesetting and colour reproduction.

6 Preparation of sales promotion plans.

7 Obtaining market research data.

8 Design and production of print brochures and literature.

Selecting suitable external support services

9   Planning, design and carrying out of direct mail.

10 Exhibition planning, design and construction.

11 Some advertising agencies also carry out public relations activities, although many prefer not to do this.

12 Rendering one, consolidated monthly account, saving you from handling a multitude of separate accounts.

How to select an agency

It is advisable to approach a fully recognised agency and to examine at least two alternative candidate agencies, if this is at all possible, to compare what they have to offer. A full picture of what the advertising agency can do for you should be obtained. The following should be expected:

- the agency should provide details of itself, its size, its turnover and should provide a list of its clients

- the agency should show examples of its work, with case histories of what it has done for other clients

- the agency should introduce the person or persons who would work on the proposed new client's business

- the agency may then perhaps be asked for its advance ideas on what to do in the present case, though, usually, advertising agencies will not provide speculative advertisements without a fee.

- lastly, the agency must clarify its usual normal terms and indicate what future costs will be.

How to use an advertising agency

There will be a fuller analysis of how to use external services at the end of the chapter (p. 140), but it is very much up to the client to use the agency in an effective way. This means giving a lead and being consistent, and includes:

1   Providing a clear and practical brief.

2. Establishing a clear and workable budget.

3. Providing a realistic timetable, and allowing enough time for work to be processed properly.

4. Carefully checking through the agency's proposals, copy, artwork, proofs, estimates, schedules and invoices.

5. Having a clear and realistic business objective against which all the agency's work may be measured.

Costs and budgets

Advertising agencies are theoretically remunerated by discounts received from the media. Most media do allow commissions.

- national press, radio, TV and magazines offer 15 per cent commissions

- local newspapers, trade and technical periodicals, and many directories offer 10 per cent

- some media, e.g. Yellow Pages, do not offer discounts.

Where the billing is large enough (a matter of judgement) but certainly over £25,000, and for larger agencies over £200,000, the agency may be willing to receive commission only.

For production, artwork and items where commission is not allowed, the agency will add on 17.65 per cent, equivalent to a 15 per cent net commission. But where the income is small, or where the workload is heavy, the agency may ask for an additional fee.

Smaller advertisers should beware of paying excessive fees, but should accept that *some* fee basis may be necessary. If so, the agency must be asked to itemise and substantiate the fee proposed.

Lastly, it is vital that the advertiser establish a firm and realistic budget for the total marketing communications programme. The agency and all other external support services must operate within this. There are two principal ways of achieving this budget: (1) on a task basis, i.e. what is required to carry out the job; or (2) a sum relative to the commercial scale of the enterprise, e.g. a percentage of annual turnover.

PUBLIC RELATIONS

PR agencies or consultancies obtain publicity coverage via a wide variety of means, often through editorial mention in the various media of communications. They are fee-based.

PR businesses are mostly separate from advertising agencies and should not be confused with them. They are distinctive in their own right.

How to find PR agencies

PR services may be found in the same way as advertising agencies – from colleagues, local businesses or trade associations. Advice and help may also be obtained from two main central bodies:

- The Institute of Public Relations, which covers all sides of public relations, including clients.
- The Public Relations Consultants Association, whose members are probably those you will wish to use.

Both these bodies will provide information and guidance, and the PRCA will provide a list of its members.

What PR consultancies offer

PR businesses can offer a wide range of facilities, and the client may choose those which are most suitable:

- editorial contacts with local and national press, TV, radio, magazines and periodicals
- press releases, circulating items of news
- editorial features, negotiating longer or more in-depth coverage
- press conferences or press facility visits
- newsletters, bulletins, house magazines
- corporate design and corporate literature, brochures etc.

- exhibitions, trade shows and fairs, launch parties, etc.
- mailings and information to contractors, customers, suppliers
- staff and internal publicity
- sponsorship work.

How PR companies operate

The PR company is usually more compact than the advertising agency, and will allocate a PR executive to handle the client's work. This executive is the key person, but may be supplemented by other staff from time to time.

How to select PR services

Here again it is advisable to compare and contrast at least two alternative PR suppliers. The following criteria should be looked for:

1. The consultancy should provide an outline of its business and experience, together with a list of clients.
2. It should show examples of its work, with case histories of what it has done.
3. It should outline its experience or media contacts in the field in question.
4. It should introduce the key PR executive who will handle the account.
5. It is common practice then to ask the PR company for a set of proposals (written document) on what it could do for the new client. These are produced on a no-commitment basis.
6. There should be a clear statement of fees and costs.

Many PR companies are general, handling any kind of client, but many specialise in particular areas or activities, such as fashion, medical products, high technology, City or financial. The client must decide if a general or specialist business is required. But if the main need is proximity, selection will be limited to those general PR companies available in the area.

Using PR services

As with advertising agencies, the client must:

- provide a clear and realistic brief
- produce a realistic and efficient budget
- operate a realistic timetable and plan in advance.

Many media, e.g. colour magazines, work many weeks in advance, and PR must operate to disciplined timetables. In addition, the PR consultancy can only work with the ammunition the client has given it. PR succeeds through a flow of ideas, news, extra items of information. So the client must always be on the alert to supply new and topical material – anything that may be newsworthy.

Costs of PR services

PR consultancies are fee-based, and fees may vary widely. So PR suppliers may differ much more than advertising suppliers. Fees should be examined closely, and must be justified. They are usually based on hours worked, i.e. an estimate of staff time, with a cost per hour. The number of hours allocated and the cost per hour must be established. There are usually two types of fee: (1) an annual continual fee, or retainer; or (2) a project fee for an *ad hoc* job.

Many consultancies charge a minimum fee to cover their costs, and £1000 per month is a bare minimum. In addition to fees, PR must cover a large variety of expenses. These include production, printing, mailing, travel, entertainment and materials.

DESIGNERS AND ART STUDIOS

Individual design or graphic work may be required, or particular types of artwork may be needed. These may be provided direct by a designer or artist. There are of course many thousands of commercial artists in Britain.

Here again, Yellow Pages or local associations can be consulted. Printers may know of artists, with whom they often closely work – ideally in your own locality. The same can be said of commercial photographers. *Advertisers' Annual* lists many specialist photographers and art studios, and ISBA and the Design Centre can advise.

It is desirable to obtain an advance quotation for work done. Charges may be worked out on an hourly, daily, half-day or session basis.

PRINTERS

Local directories will contain lists of printers. Chambers of commerce will also have information, and local businesses can usually provide names, too. Printers should be asked for examples of work done. They should then be asked to quote, including:

- a breakdown of the job
- price, with a price for extra copies
- cost of proofs
- cost of delivery.

It is desirable to see a proof and set a firm quantity to be produced. Again it is helpful to obtain at least two alternative quotations before making a decision.

MAILING HOUSES

If you conduct small levels of mailing, with small address lists, then this can be accommodated in-house. Mailing can be a potent form of contact, but if mailing numbers grow too large, then a mailing house may have to be used.

Mailing companies provide a range of services which can be combined in a package or used singly, and include:

- provision of mailing lists
- production of direct mail letters and enclosures
- matching-in of names and addresses
- inserting materials and mailing.

Certainly, a strong mailing list, or data base of addressees, is a powerful tool. At the very least, mailing houses might be used to build up a bank of names. For details of possible suppliers, advice can be obtained from the British Direct Marketing Association.

OTHER SERVICES

Local advertising agencies will be able to supply the particulars of specialist additional services. But they are also covered in specific sections of *Advertisers' Annual*, which list many categories of supplier, or again certain particular trade bodies may be contacted for advice:

1. The Market Research Society will provide a members' list, showing suppliers of particular research services.
2. The Institute of Sales Promotion will supply a list of members if sales promotion or planning or specific types of sales promotion activity are needed.
3. Exhibition stand fitters may be found in *Advertisers' Annual*.
4. Marketing Consultants may be found by consulting the Chartered Institute of Marketing or the Marketing Society.

THE MEDIA

For a complete listing of media, the best-known reference work is *British Rate and Data*, or *BRAD*. This lists press, TV, radio, cinema, poster and transport media, and gives names and addresses for each. *BRAD* is available from some libraries, but may be bought direct. The publishers also provide a companion listing of annuals and directories.

For assistance with PR and editorial contacts in the media, the standard reference is *PIMS*, which sets out the journalists for the leading media, by function or interest. It may be particularly useful to obtain press cuttings. A variety of press-cutting services are listed in *Advertisers' Annual*.

USING EXTERNAL SUPPORT SERVICES

Having located a suitable external support service and having agreed terms, you must build up a working relationship. There is an old, partly true adage: 'Clients get the work they deserve'. At any rate, the purchaser of the service is responsible for obtaining the right standard, and must control the way in which the service is developed.

The brief

Output is only as good as input. The client must brief the external service closely and precisely.

The brief may take two forms: (1) informal, general and perhaps unwritten; or (2) formal, detailed and written. In order to save disagreement later, it is advisable to put the main features of the brief in writing. If a brief is given over the telephone, or in conversation, it should be confirmed later by letter.

A typical brief would contain at least the following elements:

1. The objectives of the programme and/or the desired effect.
2. Any particular problems to overcome.
3. A definition of the target audience (who are they?) as precisely as possible.
4. The features of the product or service to be conveyed.
5. The timing of the programme, i.e. when it should take place and when the contact is expected to respond.

6 Any competitive advantages or benefits to be conveyed.

7 The precise regional scale, i.e. national, regional or local, as specifically as possible.

8 The 'tone' or atmosphere which the organisation wishes to see adopted. Each client can set his own tone, or level of image, as best fitting the corporate tradition.

9 Budget, and any cost constraints.

10 The form the proposal should take, e.g. quick return letter, media schedule, brief outline layout or detailed finished artwork, etc.

11 To whom the proposal should be made.

Once the proposal is received, it should be checked against the brief to ensure the two match up.

Progress and timing

The client must ensure that proposals from the external supplier are put into effective practice. The key to this is timing. A strict timetable must be set, and a continuing check maintained on progress. If possible, a calendar should be established, showing key actions and main dates. A typical advertising calendar might be as follows:

Activity	Date
Agency to submit proposals	4 March
Proposals agreed	8 March
Agency to produce artwork	20 March
Artwork agreed	23 March
Agency to submit first proof	3 April
Final proof agreed	7 April
Copy date, artwork to publication	9 April
Advertisement appears	15 April

Activities must work forward, e.g. advertising works to copy dates (sometimes months in advance of publication dates), or PR works to press dates. Room must be left at each stage for revision.

It is also essential that the client be shown all activities at each major stage of their development, for proper approval.

Decision-making and approvals

It is the prerogative of the client to oversee the work of the external service, and approve it as it progresses. A sensible system needs to be established for this.

First, it must be decided who within the organisation agrees the work. Usually this is done on two levels. For major plans and activities the board of directors, the managing director or senior partner approve. For routine development, the individual designated to supervise progress or to act as *de facto* marketing supervisor or publicity co-ordinator approves.

Once the work is under way, it is checked at each stage and agreed by the designated person or persons. In the process comments, suggestions and amendments may be incorporated.

It is important that agreements are given clearly and formally. This saves a great deal of misunderstanding, time and money.

Cost Control

If at all possible, an annual budget should be decided for the year's marketing programme. Costs can be set against that.

Again, a clear system is required for effective cost control:

- a cost estimate is required, per main item
- the supplier should be encouraged to obtain alternative quotations from at least two sources where sub-contractors are used, e.g. where advertising agencies use printers or photographers
- the client should try to obtain a feel for 'industry averages', to ensure that prices are in line with the market
- suppliers' invoices should be submitted quickly and in detail, and should be as per the original estimate

Selecting suitable external support services

- the final material (press space, leaflet, mailing shot, exhibition stand, etc.) should be examined, to ensure the specification is in line with the estimate as originally approved.

Every effort should be made to contain costs, especially where budgets are small. Cost-saving measures are always possible and may include the following:

1. Concentration on key items, so as to keep down fees.
2. Search for possible discounts, e.g. from newspapers.
3. Use of less expensive sub-suppliers, e.g. advertising agency use of cheaper typesetters.
4. Re-use of existing materials. Build up a bank of artwork.
5. Keeping ideas simple. For example, using a simple visual means a moderate cost for artwork; elaborate ideas usually mean extra expense.
6. Allowing plenty of time. Shortage of time leads to higher rates of expenditure, overtime costs, extra payments. The longer the time, the greater the economy.
7. Being prepared to reject cost estimates, and ask for improved prices.
8. Using suppliers who are in line with the quality and job needed. It is not necessary to use a major photographer for a small photograph in a local newspaper.

The best supplier and external support services are the ones which show most sympathy for the client's needs – not least the need for economy.

SOME HELPFUL NAMES AND ADDRESSES

Associations
Advertising Association, *see* p. 42

British Direct Marketing Association
Grosvenor Gardens House, Grosvenor Gardens, London SW1. Tel: 01 630 0361

Chartered Institute of Marketing, *see* p. 42

Direct Mail Producers Association
34 Grand Avenue, London N10 3BP. Tel: 01 883 9554

Direct Mail Sales Bureau Plc
14 Floral Street, London WC2. Tel: 01 379 7531

Incorporated Society of British Advertisers, *see* p. 42

Institute of Practitioners in Advertising
44 Belgrave Square, London W1. Tel: 01 235 7020

Institute of Public Relations, *see* p. 42

Institute of Sales Promotion
66 Pentonville Road, London N1. Tel: 01 837 5340

Market Research Society, *see* p. 42

Marketing Society, *see* p. 42

Public Relations Consultants Association
Premier House, 10 Greycoat Place, London SW1. Tel: 01 222 8866

Publications
Advertisers' Annual
British Media Publications, Windsor Court, East Grinstead House, East Grinstead, West Sussex

British Rate and Data
Maclean Hunter House, Chalk Lane, Cockfosters Road, Barnet, Herts EN4 0BU

PIMS Media Directory
PIMS London Limited, 4 St John's Place, St John's Square, London EC1M 4AH

10

HOW TO ASSESS AND ANALYSE RESULTS
by Richard N. Skinner

EDITORS' PREVIEW

Richard Skinner, BA, read classics at University College, London. He has held senior marketing appointments with Remington Rand Ltd, and GEC Reliance Ltd, where he became deputy managing director. A prolific writer, his published titles include *Launching New Products in Competitive Markets*, *How British Industry Prices*, *Pricing Strategies to Cope with Inflation*, and many others.

For many reading this chapter, the active marketing experience will have been a new one. It is essential that the results that are achieved are identified and understood. That is the only way that the marketing experience can develop into the full conviction that marketing is an essential management discipline for every type of business.

THE NEED TO MEASURE RESULTS

The concept of marketing implies a willingness to measure results and to be measured by results. Human nature, however, tends to shy away from measurement and to seek comfort in the belief that many activities do not produce results that can be assessed with any degree of precision. The professions have not been immune from this form of defensive thinking, at least where advice to clients is concerned. For if the advice given is the best possible, what else can be demanded of the adviser?

However correct such a stance may be where the product on offer is concerned, it would be unwise to extend it to any aspect of marketing. You would not be engaging in marketing without objectives that are quantifiable. Even if the aim were to stand still and maintain your business exactly as it is at present, it would be necessary to check that this was in fact happening. Any more positive plans need to be assessed and their results analysed, both to evaluate the return on effort already expended and to see what changes in direction may be required.

Granted a willingness to make assessments, the difficulties in your way are nonetheless quite real. They centre around the number of variables, the lack of a firm yardstick in many cases, and the conflict between short- and long-term considerations.

Variables

It may seem simple to look at the income of the business and see if it has increased. But what if the market for the service you are offering has increased to a greater extent? And how has the increase to income been achieved? Is it through one large transaction that is unlikely to be repeated? Is there a new pattern of business, and if so how profitable is it likely to prove? Are your competitors in some temporary difficulty from which they could recover? Have you taken the business no one else wants?

Yardsticks

What do you choose as a yardstick? Revenue, number of orders, or commissions, number of new clients, share of the available market? Whichever is chosen could produce results quite contrary to those obtained by the use of a different standard of measurement.

Short versus long term

It is often possible to maximise immediate results at the expense of longer-term factors. For example, a drastic increase in fees might be granted an unwilling acceptance by clients already committed to using your

How to assess and analyse results

services, but could have severe repercussions later. More seductively it could be believed that money spent on promotion now would not produce results for some months to come and that therefore any hasty attempt at measurement could be misleading.

Faced with these very real difficulties, it is all too easy to forgo or at least to postpone serious attempts at assessment, and to rely instead on a personal 'feel' for the health of the business. This can reflect little more than the last couple of transactions with which an individual was concerned, or the opinion of colleagues not over-anxious to tell you what you do not want to hear.

So the first step towards a disciplined assessment is a determination to measure results in whatever ways are available, recognising that any of these may have limitations. The more ways you can find of approaching an analysis of results, the more reliable a picture is likely to emerge. The experienced navigator does not rely on identifying a single mark on the horizon, but takes bearings on as many recognisable objects as possible, to narrow the inevitable zone of uncertainty which surrounds any assumed position.

In this chapter we shall look at the possibilities open for internal analysis by making use of information that is, or can be made to be, readily available. Then it will be time to examine what external research could yield for a firm which wishes to know where it now stands, whether its efforts to change direction have succeeded, and what objectives should be set for the future.

INTERNAL ANALYSIS

Orders

Without doubt the value of orders or commissions obtained will be recorded somewhere, although in some forms of professional activity the exact sum to be paid by the client is not known until the assignment is concluded. A great deal can be learned from breaking these figures down rather than leaving them lumped together.

The number of orders received each month or each quarter needs to be logged, as well as the value of each order. Once this is done, a picture emerges of the business as a whole. It may consist entirely of small assignments, the average size of which is fairly constant, or at the other extreme the business might be built on a very few large orders obtained at irregular intervals. More likely there is a mixture.

The mix needs to be examined critically, because it is unlikely that all sizes of order are equally profitable or equally welcome. One objective of the marketing plan may well be to encourage orders of the right size for the firm to handle. Whether this is done by pricing or by some form of promotion, we need to watch the analysis of orders carefully to see that we are moving in the right direction.

In addition to the *size* of an order, the *product* involved can be analysed. It is likely that a professional practice will have a number of 'products' to offer, which again vary in their relative *profitability*. Control over this aspect of the business may help to improve the use of skilled time; it may also serve to establish the image of the practice in the eyes of potential clients.

It cannot be assumed that these aspects are fully understood without analysis, even by those closest to them. In fact that very closeness sometimes serves to conceal the importance to a business of orders which are not especially prominent or glamorous. The question to ask is whether you or your partners really know how many orders, of what value, are being received for each category of business, and how profitable or desirable each category is. Unless regular statistics are being kept and costs attributed to each category, opportunities for moving the business in the direction you most want may be slipping away.

Often the form in which information is available can lead to ambiguity in allotting orders to this or that category. This means that it is not a job to give to a junior employee, at least until all such difficulties have been resolved. It is, after all, your business, and it will pay you to have a first-hand appreciation of exactly what the figures mean and how they are compiled.

If the business is not confined to one clearly defined geographical area, a further analysis by *area* is needed to see that opportunities are not being neglected, or to identify geographical problems. To this can be added in some cases an analysis by *market sector* or type of client. Sometimes this is a corollary of the product supplied but not always. A bank may lend money to industrial clients and the product, in terms of the money itself or the interest it earns, is much the same in all cases. The clients are, however, highly differentiated and represent a wide spread of activity, each sector of which contains its own risks.

Each of the factors discussed so far might have featured in a marketing campaign to secure business of this or that kind. Efforts might, for example, have been made to attract new types of client (the market sector approach) or more small to medium-sized orders. An analysis of orders will not necessarily reveal whether the campaign has been successful, because you may have benefited simultaneously from a market upsurge or from a competitor's advertising programme. But the figures so far discussed will at least give an indication and will show quite clearly if your marketing has *not* worked.

With specific campaigns in mind it pays to analyse as far as possible the *source* of each order. Can it be traced to an introduction from an existing client, to a search of reference books, or to any specific promotional activity in which you have been engaged (e.g. a seminar)? Such distinctions may not be easy to make after a long period of negotiation. It will therefore pay to identify the source at the time an enquiry is received.

To summarise so far, an analysis of orders in terms of:

- number
- size
- product
- profitability
- geographical area
- market sector
- source

will do a great deal to define the type of business you are obtaining, to identify trends and to check the success of promotional efforts.

It is an activity for a senior executive in the first instance, because it is necessary to have confidence in the reliability of figures on which important decisions may depend. Once established, the figures should receive a regular review, not simply to assess past results, but to see what changes in direction may be appropriate.

Enquiries and conversions

A record of the number of enquiries received is clearly desirable, and will in most cases already exist. Fluctuations in number may reflect market trends as well as promotional activity, and are often an early warning of the need to increase marketing activity. It is, however, necessary to define what constitutes an enquiry. Most firms receive a number of approaches from potential or existing clients based on recommendation or knowledge of work done in the past or on a generally disseminated reputation for handling certain types of business. Such enquiries form the hard core of prospective orders on which the firm depends.

There are also enquiries for information about the services on offer which are not related to any specific projects, but rather to a desire to have on hand the relevant information in case of future need. What the enquirer wants in these instances is literature for retention rather than help right now. Of course it is not always easy to distinguish between a general and a specific interest, but if you have promoted your firm and invited people to send for information about your services, it will pay to list replies to such a campaign separately and to count as firm enquiries only those customers who respond to your literature with a request for action of some kind or another.

If the business is such that *quotations* are expected before orders are placed, it is worth comparing numbers of enquiries received to numbers of quotations. Some key ratios can then be developed:

- enquiries received: quotations despatched
- quotations despatched: orders received

These ratios can be further sub-divided to parallel the categories under which orders have been listed. Thus the value of quotations can be compared with the value of orders received, and similar comparisons can be made for each product and each market sector. It may then be possible to define categories where the success rate is higher or lower than elsewhere, and to seek reasons why.

If, for example, you are achieving a better conversion ratio for small orders than for large, it may indicate that your pricing needs attention, although this cannot be assumed without some thought given to whether customers 'shop around' more when more money is at stake. If, as is sometimes the case, you are obtaining relatively more orders for products which are less profitable than others, you may again want to adjust charges, or to look at ways of promoting more profitable offerings. In each case it is a study of the conversion ratio which points to a need for further and deeper consideration.

How to assess and analyse results

Another benefit of looking at enquiries and conversions related to orders is that the number and type of enquiries being received can provide the basis of a forecast of business in the immediate future. If 20 per cent of enquiries are known to become orders, for example, then you are better able to predict the likely order intake, given that a view of the time it takes an enquiry to mature can be formed. In some professions and for certain types of activity the time delay may be very short. Some services are needed in a hurry if at all. But architects, financial advisers and management consultants in many aspects of their work may experience a considerable time gap before decisions are made.

The analysis of conversions can in such circumstances pose a problem, because obviously you will want to work on the most up-to-date ratio, and yet there may be a number of enquiries which have not so far matured, but may very well do so in time. There are in general two ways of handling this.

First, a moving average of quotations and orders may be kept so that over, say, 12 months you know the value of orders has been £3,500,000 while the value of quotations was £28,000,000. The conversion percentage is therefore 12.5. Next month these figures are updated to give new totals and a new percentage. This method generally produces a sound indication of trends in conversion, but the monthly figures reflect a comparison between last month's quotations and last month's orders, which may have stemmed from quotations made not last month but at any time over the last year or so. Large orders or large quotations occurring in any one month can therefore cause some distortion, which may have to be allowed for in making calculations, or at least annotated.

As an alternative, or in addition, it could be worth listing all quotations and marking those which become orders, so that the success rate in recent months can be examined. In instances where there is a known time-lag, the most recent quotations cannot be expected to show a complete conversion ratio, but may indicate a trend.

As the object of this exercise is to be able to predict future business, as much or more may be gained from breaking conversion statistics down into product and market sector categories as from the overall figures described above. You may then be better able to estimate the resources you will need to handle the business coming your way.

Specific campaigns

Specific marketing effort may not always produce easily identifiable results. You may even be told that you should not anticipate immediate enquiries stemming from a campaign to establish an image or simply to get your name more widely recognised. Nevertheless money has been spent and a measurable return on it should be expected.

In some instances it may be necessary to look outside the firm for an indication of success or failure, but first there are a number of actions which can be taken internally. Before a campaign is initiated, everyone on the staff ought to know what is about to take place. This not only boosts morale, but enables every employee to assist in logging enquiries against whatever it was that stimulated them. A simple question to a potential client making an initial contact by telephone is often all that is needed. It will pay to number each campaign and to enter this number against every enquiry associated with the campaign. Thus the enquiry book might show an entry '1069/DM2', enquiry number 1069 being associated with the second direct mail shot of your current campaign.

When an order follows, this also needs to be traced back to the original enquiry to see what indication of source is available. However simple this may sound, it is common to find organisations with no real means of tracing orders back to source, and thus with only a hazy notion of whether or not their promotional efforts are being rewarded.

Of course advertising cannot always be coded as easily as direct mail shots or, where appropriate, exhibition enquiries. Where an advertisement carries a coupon or a journal operates a reply-card system, it is simple enough, but an image-building advertisement may not come in this category, and neither may the editorial obtained via a press release. This is where your telephonist or any member of staff can help by a question such as 'May I ask where you found our name?'

If publicity is on a large enough scale, it may be worth considering the *yellow telephone approach*. This was so named after an effort to discover just how many enquiries Yellow Pages were producing. The advertisement inserted gave the company's name, but with a special telephone number, rather than that of the switchboard. A direct line was installed and all calls received were logged so that enquiries related to Yellow Pages could be separated from those coming from other sources. The same technique can be used for any advertising campaign, and does not appear to create any problems in subsequent dealings, since

How to assess and analyse results

once literature or letters have been sent, the potential customer naturally uses the number on the letterhead.

In attempting to measure editorial publicity (e.g. the result of a press release) there are special problems which need special solutions. There is little doubt that this is one of the best media open to the professional adviser, and especially to the smaller firm, in communicating with potential clients and establishing an image. The problem is that there is no real control over what is printed, so that it is not always possible to trace enquiries originating from what the client sees as editorial. The client may not even remember where and when he or she first saw your name in print.

As a consequence PR agencies have tended to fight shy of measurement. At their worst they may be content to produce reports detailing the efforts they are making on your behalf without attempting to quantify the results they are obtaining. As a marked improvement on this they may use a press-cutting service to collect everything which has appeared in print. If this is a substantial enough compendium, it will appear impressive, and is certainly useful in showing your own staff that the firm is getting attention in the press. The question that it begs is one of quality. Press 'mileage' may be of little value if the mentions you get are in journals your clients are most unlikely to read.

One way of overcoming difficulties of this kind is to use an *a,b,c, system* of rating. At regular intervals you and the person responsible for placing press releases sit down to examine press cuttings received since your last review. Each is given a rating somewhat on these lines:

a = Interesting article in a journal of importance, likely to influence prime prospects.

b = Shorter mention in a good journal, or interesting article in a less important journal.

c = Straightforward 'product' mention (e.g. in a press survey of available services).

d = Mention in a poor or inappropriate journal.

x = Unfavourable mention in any context.

It is then possible to chart progress from one period to another, to encourage the creation of more *a* and *b* articles and to reduce wasted or misguided effort. Naturally the judgements made are subjective and qualitative in their nature, but they may be quite valid if the same people make them each time and on a consistent basis. The point is that some form of measurement is attempted, and that in itself is a great stimulus to improvement. Of course, if enquiries can be attributed more directly to any press release, that should be done in parallel, and the results discussed at the same regular meetings.

Meetings to examine the statistics that all forms of internal analysis have produced are important, once you have established a systematic marketing programme. Enquiries of all types for all your different 'products', orders in their various categories, conversion ratios and the more subjective forms of assessment just discussed are worth a regular review with everyone concerned in marketing the firm's services. The timing of review meetings is important. They may be frequent when a campaign is in progress, but once a month may well be sufficient where basic figures are concerned. The purpose of such meetings is not just to communicate and enthuse, but to produce specific action points and changes of direction where necessary. Enough time has therefore to elapse to enable trends to become clear, as well as to avoid devaluing the meeting by holding it too frequently.

Limitations of internal analysis

The main weakness of internal analysis is that it is historical and essentially quantitative. It provides facts and figures, but you have to interpret them. If numbers of orders and enquiries are rising, does this mean you are getting a larger share of the available business, or that the business as a whole is growing? You may even be obtaining a smaller share than previously and yet your internal figures will show an upward trend. Again, if an individual product is showing an increase, your statistics will not tell you why, or whether it could be doing even better. To answer these questions, and to make longer-term projections, we need to look outside the firm to the market in which it operates.

EXTERNAL RESEARCH

Quantitative

The first question that might be asked is how much business is available? This is, however, not so easy to answer, because there may be a greater potential for the services offered than has yet been realised. In fact the more imaginative and creative forms of marketing are looking for that potential rather than simply battling it out with competitors to obtain a greater share of what is currently available.

You can make your own estimates of the potential, using whatever figures are published publicly or within the profession. The numbers of possible clients and the frequency with which they may need advice or assistance can form the basis of a potential figure which can be considerably greater than the business currently being done.

Nevertheless the size of the business transacted each year is a good yardstick of your own performance. Figures are sometimes collected by professional associations or published in journals. If your competitors' accounts are published, they will give an indication of the volume of business each firm is doing, although some interpretation may be necessary if a competitor also transacts types of business other than your own.

If it is desired to go further and research the market to get an up-to-date picture of the total sales volume of all participants and an indication of individual market shares, research agencies will handle assignments of this kind; but it is likely to be a costly exercise, because of the size of sample needed to produce statistical accuracy, especially if any breakdown of the figures is required. Sometimes agencies produce 'syndicated' studies in which you might participate, which can reduce the cost of research considerably. Nevertheless field research of this kind is used more often to establish a starting point for marketing than to measure results on a continuous basis. The cost normally precludes its regular use by the smaller firm.

In summary then the main lines of approach to quantitative research are:

- Assessment of potential from published statistics
- Assessment of total annual business from:

professional or trade association figures
surveys in journals
syndicated research studies
one-off market surveys.

Qualitative

Qualitative research may be done on a one-off basis at more modest expense, and can be sharp-angled to give you not only a measure of your success but a sometimes quite detailed guide to the direction further promotion should take. It is less expensive than quantitative studies, because what is provided is relative information that does not have to be grossed up to provide accurate estimates of market shares or volumes of business. If, for example, you want to know how your clients or potential clients regard you and your main competitors, this information is more easily gathered than figures on how much people have spent or intend to spend on the services you offer. Furthermore it is often possible to get reliable returns from a smaller sample than would be needed to illuminate financial aspects, especially if a market is widespread and purchases are infrequent.

The type of information which it would be useful to know might include:

1 AWARENESS   How well known are the services you and your competitors offer? How well known are you and your competitors?

2 REPUTATION   How do clients or potential clients rate you and your competitors against a number of factors, which might include promptness in handling assignments, reliability of advice given, cost, ability to communicate, clarity of reports, etc.?

3 CUSTOMERS' BUYING PRACTICES   How do clients choose a professional adviser? What criteria are important to them? How do they obtain information on services available? What journals do they read?

4 COMPETITORS' SELLING METHODS   Have clients been approached by competitors? If so, what methods were used? How did they react to them?

The methods that a research expert would employ to find answers to these questions would preserve the anonymity of both sponsor and respondents. The skill lies in constructing a questionnaire which is short, produces unambiguous replies and can be answered on the spot without reference to files. Obviously care needs to be taken in selecting a random sample and in obtaining interviews with the right person to answer the particular questions asked.

It is never easy to generalise about research costs, but £5,000 could buy a meaningful amount of qualitative research, whereas it would be unlikely to go far towards funding a one-off quantitative field research which included market size and competitors' shares. This means that for many firms qualitative research is repeatable more frequently than would be the case with quantified market studies. The advantages are considerable. Market research can provide:

- a definition of the starting point for promotional effort
- a guide to the direction such effort might take and, if repeated at the end of a major campaign
- a measure of the success of specific campaigns.

You will thus be able to see whether potential clients have become more aware of your existence, how they rate you in comparison with your main competitors and whether your promotional campaign has made any tangible impact.

Refinements include the possibility of checking at a later date to see how well the message you have been trying to communicate has remained in the minds of respondents, and thus to gauge how frequently you should plan to promote the firm's image.

INTERNAL AND EXTERNAL MEASUREMENTS IN COMBINATION

Internal analysis has to be established at the outset to make any sense at all of marketing. A great deal can be achieved by a detailed analysis of enquiries and orders, and by recording and assessing the results of specific campaigns. Even activities which are longer-term in their nature and therefore harder to measure, e.g. PR campaigns, can still be assessed on a comparative scale.

The danger is that although internal analysis may show that you are doing well, it may not show how well you could do. It will certainly indicate if any campaign has failed or if any product is not performing as it should, but it may not tell you why this is so.

To answer these questions as much knowledge as possible should be gathered about the size of the market you are addressing and how it is segmented. This implies the use of external figures, and where these are not available, full-scale market studies or a share in syndicated research may be worth while. More immediately and at less cost it should be possible to research clients' awareness and opinions of all the firms competing in your market and to gather useful information on the promotional approaches most likely to succeed.

If this sounds a formidable array of techniques to be deployed simply to measure what is being achieved, it is indeed. Most of the methods discussed can, however, be built into routines based on information available internally, augmented by external research before and after any major promotional campaign. Success is after all more likely to come to the firm which knows what it is doing and can react positively and quickly to changes in the market-place.

11

MARKETING IN PRACTICE FOR CONSULTING ENGINEERS AND OTHER PROFESSIONAL ADVISERS IN THE INDUSTRIAL SECTOR

Part 1 by Stephen Morse
Part 2 by Nigel Dearsly

EDITORS' PREVIEW

This chapter is in two parts – the first part by Stephen Morse, the author of Chapter 2. He begins to demonstrate the marketing discipline at work in practical environments.

Part Two is a true-life example of the marketing discipline in action. Nigel Dearsly, the managing director of Salamander Estates, a property development and investment company, gives an example which encompasses many of the marketing concepts that have been presented in earlier chapters.

PART 1 INDUSTRIAL MARKETING TECHNIQUES

Colin McIver says:

> The management principle, attitude or what you will that embodies the basic marketing philosophy . . . can be applied just as usefully *mutatis*

mutandis to the marketing of a service which cannot be manufactured, packaged and exposed for sale in a supermarket gondola. Just how much of a conventional product marketing technology needs to be mutated and how much can be carried over holus bolus is the only really interesting question.[1]

Three major differences are addressed in looking at the practice of marketing advice to industrial companies. Thus many professional advisers whose main thrust is towards individuals are excluded from this illustration. Other considerations affect such notable advisers as solicitors, architects and estate agents, whose market can certainly be as volatile and irrational as it is believed the shopper in the supermarket is. Recently many financial advisers have also started down the same road. But this chapter looks at the 'industrial market' from the point of view of management and business consultants and firms of consulting engineers.

The *first* difference is in the complexity of the market. Even defining the word 'market' in such a way that the majority of both purchasers and providers of advisory services would agree is difficult. For example, there is a computer market – those who have a need for and will buy computers – and there is a hospital market. Here we have defined 'market' in terms of what is sold (computers) and in terms of type of establishment (hospitals, who buy hospital supplies but who might buy computers, too). Sometimes the word is used to refer to demand – 'not much of a market for method study these days'. For this chapter 'market' refers primarily to actual and potential clients (buyers).

Thus the market is extremely varied both in its composition – the size and type of industrial company – and in its requirement for advice. (For example, within the Richmond Group, an association of some seventy independent management consultants, no less than 122 'fields of activity and experience' were identified, and additionally some thirty-five industries where the group's members had special experience.) One needs only to think of the infinite variety of different industrial and other organisations in the UK, let alone those in the rest of the European Community and then in the rest of the world.

This market is also served by a very wide range of different advisers – not only management and business consultants, but also the wide range of financial advisers, legal counsel, scientific and engineering consultants, advertising agencies, and public relations image-makers. These are organised in firms and practices of different sizes. Large companies, such as the large accounting firms, the top ten of which had a turnover of more than £1,000 million in 1986–87, receive some 40 per cent of this income from management consulting. Such companies embrace a very wide spectrum of different disciplines and 'expertise' (see Chapter 2). Also in this 'market-place' are medium-sized specialist advisers (e.g. computing software), small local practices and single freelancers who occasionally operate in loose associations.

Such a general 'market-place' confusion demands from individual firms and practices a disciplined *approach to marketing information* and research. The following cases exemplify three aspects of this approach:

1. A small Dutch consulting engineer (Ingenieurs bureau) became aware that business was being lost because project managers were not aware of the strength of their relationships with architects, clients and other decision-makers. The managing director decided to undertake some training of project managers based on the different relationships needed towards different members of the decision-making unit (DMU). Project managers were first asked to identify:

   Users of the firm's services

   Influencers of the decision to use the firm's services, such as architects, designers, other consultants

   Decision-makers – the clients and their agents

   Buyers – those holding the financial purse-strings

   Gatekeepers – those with control over access to clients and architects.

This information was collected and indexed, and not only used as the basis of training but also for further sales and sales promotion activity.

2. An engineering consultancy practice (400–500 employees), which had suffered because of cuts in its traditional work for the Ministry of Defence, was forced to look for new clients. Two aspects of its approach were (a) assembling all the information about existing contracts with non-MOD clients, and creating a marketing co-ordination committee to establish 'intelligence-gathering about the existing client base', and (b) investigating what information was available within the firm (from ex-employees, or those with other levels of contact) about the

industries (such as steel, gas and water) which seemed the most promising market areas for the firm to tackle.

3   A growing software engineering consultancy needed to grow faster and decided to check on existing clients, by industry and location, and then to search for 'clones' within the same industry (e.g. machine-tool manufacturers) and in carefully chosen geographical areas, by a judicious use of Kompass. This provided the firm with an address and telephone list which gave it a focused starting point.

The second major difference is that it is extremely difficult to discover from the organisational structure of a management consulting or consulting engineer firm what its 'product' is. Indeed in many cases the structure is a loosely connected 'project matrix' form like Figure 11.1.

PROJECTS	SPECIALISMS			
	Engineering	Acoustics	Flow Models	Software
A				
B				
C				
D				
E				
F				

FIGURE 11.1 Project matrix form

As regards the three examples discussed above, the most difficult was the large consulting engineer practice, example 2.

The firm had expanded on the basis of projects which the Minstry of Defence had in many cases initiated. For these projects it had been necessary to take on specialists in many fields, e.g. if you are designing a warship, then you need not only experts in propulsion but also specialists in computerised weapon system controls. When there was a downturn in business owing to a reduction in MOD work, confusion arose as to where to start looking for new business. In a report to the board an outside consultant wrote: 'It is not too unkind to suggest that the view is that "we have these specialist skills; there must be someone somewhere who needs them".' At the same time the different services of the firm included:

- advising on design
- auditing design
- designing to solve problems
- assisting with problem-solving
- creating prototypes
- writing operating manuals
- creating 'software'
- providing working drawings
- advising on 'hardware' selection
- making 'hardware'.

Many of the 'products' which were thus created (and which also included administering training programmes and selling electronic hardware) were justified on grounds of profitability. It became therefore more and more tempting to be 'all things to all men', when in fact there was a need to tackle the other axis of the matrix (Figure 11.1) and try to acquire *industrial* projects which could be operated in the same way as MOD projects.

The Dutch consulting engineer (example 1) had less trouble in this regard, though he was also organised in the same way. He appointed a commercial director with responsibility for selling projects which made use of the company's technical specialities.

The software engineering consultancy (example 3), however, was faced with the difficulties afflicting example 2, in some cases in a more acute form, in that 'products' *were* 'individuals'. Nevertheless the appointment of a new marketing manager allowed a careful analysis to be made of the firm's strengths and weaknesses, and therefore of the kind of work which the firm could undertake competitively (see the Bateson Matrix, p. 22).

The third difference between the marketing of professional advice and conventional industrial or consumer goods arises in the area of the organisation of 'selling'. Faced with a downturn in the forward billings, managing directors are wont to say to their managers 'Go out and sell!' This knee-jerk reaction, however, raises two questions: 'Should we sell?' and 'Who should sell?'

'Should we sell?' is answered in three ways: it is said (1) that professionals shouldn't need to sell, since their special expertise is such that they can simply wait for needy customers to approach them (like doctors or lawyers or accountants); (2) that professionals are not good at selling, for by definition, the typical extroversion and communication skills required in selling are not part of the professional's toolbox; or (3) that sales people are born not made, so that attempting to train, say, professional engineers in selling skills is pointless.

The second question (Who should sell?) is asked only when the first has been in one way or another neutralised; and in the three cases outlined above there seemed to be three answers – each of which has pros and cons. The first answer is that *everyone should sell*, the reasoning *in favour* of this being that everyone is in contact with the major source (up to 75 per cent) of future business, and the client sees the adviser who will be carrying out the work. *Against* this reasoning is the view that people tend to avoid doing what they dislike or are bad at – indeed in some cases will find other more urgent/important uses for their time. In addition, successful sales people are not necessarily successful operators or advisers: they tend to sell their solutions too vigorously.

The second answer is that *only senior partners/managers should sell*, since senior partners or consultants have the knowledge and experience built up over time to enable them to know what should be offered to clients. They are also nearer to the 'corporate strategy centre', and those making strategic decisions should be aware of the strengths and weaknesses of the product. The more cynical of the 'labourers in the vineyard' have been heard to mutter that 'it gives them something to do!' Once again *the other side* holds the view that the fact that they are experienced senior partners or good managers does not make them sensitive sales people, that they tend to sell what *they* have done before rather than what the client needs or wants, and that they tend to sell the competences and specialisms that just at that moment 'happen to be available'.

The third answer is that a *special selling group* should be created: sales people should be recruited and they should do the selling job. The reasoning here is that selling is a skill and, because sales are so important to growth and prosperity, specialists who can concentrate on getting the most profitable clients should be engaged. Additionally both quantity and focus of the sales effort can be controlled. The main arguments *against* are that sales people 'always sell what we haven't got or can't profitably produce', that they do not know enough about the product to convince the client, and that the client in any case wants to see and talk to the 'operator'.

There is no right way to solve this problem. Each of the examples above took a different route. Example 1 chose the 'everyone should sell' solution, example 2 the senior consultant/manager way and example 3 is in the process of appointing a sales force. They have, however, one thing in common – a central marketing or commercial department which plans and co-ordinates the approach to clients.

PART 2 HOW A MARKETING APPROACH CAN BE OF BENEFIT

Salamander Estates Limited is a property development and investment company with a small team of executive directors, none of whom has received any formal marketing training. None the less, they believe the basic principles of marketing are fundamental to the success of any business. Marketing for the Salamander executive team starts in front of the shaving mirror first thing in the morning. It is a discipline that affects the way the individual members of the board present themselves, and therefore the company, from dawn until dusk, from the selection of the right tie to the preparation for a meeting and the conduct of that meeting.

Marketing is seen as an all-embracing concept of assessing what the customer requires, and setting out to try and satisfy those requirements at every possible level – even to the extent of recognising needs that customers themselves may not have identified. Differentiating Salamander from its competitors is the key to the company's approach, even if it means on occasions taking risks. However, one principle is never forgotten, the simple adage that the customer is always king.

These principles are even applied by the Salamander executive team when selecting their own professional consultants. The senior partner of a well-known firm of architects once made a simple statement at a cocktail party which greatly attracted a Salamander director. He said that good architecture need not cost a great deal of money. By this the architect meant that well-designed buildings need not be more expensive than poorly designed buildings, and that the clients of that firm of architects would benefit from better-designed buildings at no extra cost. The crucial point of the statement was that the architect understood what his clients required.

That architectural practice and Salamander Estates have since undertaken a great deal of work together, and the principles of that statement by the senior partner have held good throughout. The very simple business philosophy of knowing what the customer needed, and expressing the ability to satisfy that need, has dominated the Salamander team's approach to the way it conducts its business, and expects other professional advisers to conduct theirs.

An example of a successful development project undertaken some years ago by Salamander and the circumstances surrounding that project are contained in the following story. One morning a Salamander director received a telephone call from the manager of the operating subsidiary of a company that was a tenant of a small building which formed part of Salamander's investment portfolio. It was evident from his tone of voice that the caller was slightly agitated, although the purpose of the call was simply to arrange a meeting to discuss the tenant company's particular property needs. When the meeting took place, the manager explained that he had been despatched by his colleagues to negotiate the best possible terms for release from his company's commitment to the lease of the building he occupied – a lease that had a good many years to run. He was worried that Salamander, as landlords, would make the release either difficult or expensive for his company and he felt certain that if Salamander was really obstructive, it could frustrate his main objective, which was to move to larger and more modern accommodation better suited to his high-technology business. The directors of his parent company had given him some very severe budgetary constraints and he knew that there was a serious risk he could not achieve his ambition to move if anything went wrong at any stage of the negotiations. If his plans were to proceed, he had to secure a release from his existing commitment at a very low figure and acquire new premises at realistic rental levels, probably below those levels prevailing in the open market. By any standards, he had a difficult assignment.

As the meeting developed, and the manager of the tenant company realised that he had found a sympathetic ear in the form of the Salamander director, he relaxed and began to describe in ever greater detail the nature of his problem. Gradually the Salamander director began to recognise that he enjoyed some particular and unique advantages which put Salamander in a very special position in this negotiation.

First of all, Salamander knew more about the tenant's problem than anyone else – more than the board of the tenant company, and certainly more than Salamander's competitors. The Salamander director also knew that his company was likely to be the only one capable of solving the tenant's problems, as he knew that if he could find an appropriate site which, with Salamander's skill as a professional developer it could develop profitably, it could afford to absorb whatever financial risk there might be in releasing the tenant from its obligations to its existing building. At the same time, Salamander alone had the opportunity to permit the tenant to remain in occupation until the new building was ready, and while this would inevitably delay the move longer than originally planned, this delay was more than compensated for in the eyes of the tenant by the certainty that a new, customised building would be waiting for occupation in due course.

What the manager of the tenant company and his colleagues had not seen were the constituent parts of their problem as being linked. They had seen a series of separate problems without the collective opportunity which Salamander could uniquely recognise and exploit.

At the end of the meeting, the Salamander director proposed to the tenant that Salamander would find the tenant company a suitable site, build it a building specifically designed to meet its needs – with the high-technology image it required – charge them a new rent below present market levels and release it from its existing lease commitment at no cost. In the meantime the tenant could continue to occupy its existing building until the new building was ready and at the present rental level. The manager from the tenant company left Salamander's offices with a broad smile on his face and the confidence to inform his board members that he had an answer to a problem which they had previously believed was difficult, if not insoluble. All the Salamander director had done was listen to the tenant's story, place himself in the tenant's shoes and tailor a solution to his needs with the special knowledge that if Salamander's assumptions about its own business were correct, it could make a substantial profit from answering the tenant company's problem. Like architecture, good development need not cost a great deal of money.

While the tenant's problem appeared to be over when the manager left Salamander's offices, Salamander's own problems were just beginning. The director had had an idea which still required some action if it was going to be converted into a successful commercial venture. However, he had a ready-made tenant for a new development if he could find a suitable site; and, if he could find that site and procure an attractive building on it, Salamander would have an interesting package to sell to a property investment organisation, provided it was properly presented.

The outcome of the story was that, within a week of the meeting with the tenant, Salamander received a further telephone call from the manager of the tenant company, although this time his tone was quite different. He invited the Salamander director to meet his group chairman and chief executive, as they had received the report on the outcome of the earlier meeting with such enthusiasm that they wanted to discuss the possibility of moving the whole of the group's activities from its existing premises to a new major campus if Salamander would be interested in helping them! This they did within 18 months of the initial diffident telephone call.

The high-technology company was delighted with the outcome and its business has prospered in its new accommodation. Salamander made a very satisfactory profit from the leasing of the new buildings and the sale of the completed investment, and the final sugar-coating to the story was that it re-let the premises which the tenant vacated to excellent new tenants and at significantly higher rental levels.

Now what has this true story to do with marketing? The simple answer is everything. Certainly, it does not contain market research, sales management, press releases, television appearances, advertising features or even a sales brochure. However, what it does contain is the essential element of understanding the client's problem and using one's skill and knowledge to overcome that problem for reward. What is that if it is not marketing in its purest sense?

The manager of the tenant company had not asked for a meeting with Salamander to obtain a new building; on the contrary he had come cap in hand specifically to negotiate the best terms for the release of his company from its obligations to its existing building. He believed that he was the messenger of bad news and he had no idea at all that he was in fact about to do his landlord a major favour. He did not possess sufficient knowledge of Salamander's business to appreciate the possibilities, nor at the time could he see beyond his own particular domestic problems.

In the many years that the directors of Salamander have been practising at the commercial end of their profession, it has been their frequent experience that clients have sought advice on what they perceived to be their particular problem, when in reality the problem on which they should have been seeking advice was quite a different one, had they had the knowledge to realise it. On the other side of the coin, when Salamander has sought advice from professional consultants, those consultants all too often have a preconceived idea of the advice Salamander ought to be seeking and have therefore been unable or unwilling to give the advice Salamander has actually requested. Sometimes there is a degree of superiority in the way professionals go about their business, coupled with an unwillingness to place themselves in the client's shoes.

To take this idea further, the board of Salamander has developed a positive strategy of setting aside management time to consider the possible direction in which their clients' and customers' needs might move in future. Sometimes Salamander has even been able to develop a product or service ahead of its particular market and at a time when the potential customer might not himself have appreciated that he needed a product or service which was on offer. This approach to marketing is commonplace in the world of consumer goods and services, but it is all too rare among the professions. Directing client demand can be an exciting and profitable business.

Perhaps the first lesson of marketing is to take time out from one's busy routine work schedule to think about the direction of one's business, but in particular the present and future needs of one's clients and customers.

REFERENCES

1 McIver, Colin *Marketing for Managers* (Professional Perspectives in Marketing, 1972)

FURTHER READING

Holtz, H. *How to Succeed as an Independent Consultant* (John Wiley, 1983)

Wilson, A. *The Marketing of Professional Services* (McGraw-Hill, 1972)

12

MARKETING IN PRACTICE FOR ACCOUNTANTS
by Keith Lindsay

EDITORS' PREVIEW

Keith Lindsay is marketing director of Moores Rowland, a 'Top 20' firm of accountants and business advisers. Moores Rowland offers a full range of professional services to all sizes of business, and is a founder member of Moores Rowland International, the eleventh largest accountancy association in the world.

Keith Lindsay's very positive approach to the subject of marketing will leave the reader in little doubt that Moores Rowland's position in the 'Top 20' was not achieved by accident.

INTRODUCTION

When practising accountants read articles on marketing, they are often quick to comment that it all makes perfect sense in theory. But how can these theories be applied by partners and staff who have more than enough on their plates servicing existing clients?

The aim of this chapter is to show that such theories are entirely relevant to professional accountants' day-to-day activities, and to provide practical guidance to partners who wish to develop their practice using marketing techniques. It has partners' scepticism very much in mind, as it is based on the experience of applying marketing practices to a successful medium-sized firm of accountants. If any part of what follows smacks of theory, it is because that theory has worked!

These comments are directed primarily at the smaller firm which does not have the benefit of a full-time marketing specialist. The tone is intentionally positive, because of a firmly held belief in the merits of a market-led approach to practice development. It is recognised, however, that not everyone shares this view, so likely objections are addressed and, it is to be hoped, satisfied.

Anyone trying to introduce the techniques that fall within the description 'marketing' to a firm should never assume they are entirely new to that firm. Virtually all these techniques will already be in use, often very successfully. They may simply be known by different terms, such as 'client service standards' or 'business development'. However, where there is no conscious market orientation, there will almost certainly be room to impose a more effective structure to control these activities, and to direct them where they will have the greatest effect. When that has been achieved, it will have proved the merits of marketing – a discipline to help partners and staff use to optimum effect the limited time they have available for business development.

IMPORTANCE OF A PLANNED APPROACH

Any marketing plan, or plans, will be complementary but subsidiary to the firm's business and financial objectives. This of course presupposes that the firm has put together a business plan to guide and direct its future activities. In many cases the two can effectively be combined so long as the partners and managers charged with formulating such plans recognise the full range of management activities which fall under the heading 'marketing', and avoid the pitfall of downgrading marketing to include simply promotional activities and techniques.

The number of marketing plans that need to be produced will depend on the range of markets served. For example, a medium-sized firm with several offices will need individual plans for each office. If that firm also has teams of specialists, say in management consultancy and corporate finance, these teams also will need to formulate their own business or marketing plans.

Excessive reliance on the planning process will inevitably lead to charges of bureaucracy and rigidity. Such reservations can be overcome quickly by pointing out the principal advantages of a planned approach, namely that it:

- specifies at the outset what activities need to be undertaken to achieve the objectives agreed
- helps to direct staff and other scarce resources to the areas where their efforts will have greatest effect
- forms a concrete basis for reviewing progress towards objectives, so that variations can be identified and the reasons recognised
- provides the basis for effective co-ordination of the different parts of the organisation, thus avoiding duplication of effort.

Which person or team should be given responsibility for preparing such a plan or plans, and monitoring the success with which they are put into effect, is one of the first decisions which the firm must take. When selecting those responsible, it is worth remembering that the preparation of a plan of this nature will demand time and concentration, so the authors should be freed as far as possible from other short-term commitments.

Partners and staff who have the chance to put forward their own ideas for inclusion are more likely to take an active role in implementing the plan than those who have not. One way to enlist support is for the author of the plan to circulate an early draft with a request for comments and suggestions by a specified date. He can then refine the final plan in line with the comments received.

A word of caution: there is absolutely no point in spending time preparing and discussing a plan if it does not include explicit procedures by which the success of the activities detailed in the plan can be monitored and reviewed, so that the plan can where necessary be amended.

WHICH MARKETS TO CONSIDER

The 'ideal' way of determining the future development of the firm – in marketing terms at least – is first to identify all the different types of clients that the firm either wishes to retain and develop if existing clients, or attract if potential clients. The next stages are, for each type, to attempt to determine their specific needs, the competition the firm is likely to face if it tries to attract and service that client type, and then, on the basis of an analysis of their needs and of the competition, attempt to determine as objectively as possible the firm's ability to service those needs at a profit, based on existing internal resources.

This is the 'ideal' way, and where possible should be followed. The strength of this approach is that it concentrates on what the market needs rather than what the firm can provide, and forces the firm to consider a wide range of alternatives rather than concentrating only on what it currently does well. However, to undertake this kind of exercise thoroughly, the firm must consider many potential markets that for various reasons it may decide to reject as potential targets. When operating under time constraints, or perhaps in the face of a certain amount of scepticism from some partners as to the benefits of the exercise, this may seem a relatively inefficient use of time.

An alternative starting point is to identify as accurately as possible which of the firm's existing clients produce the most profitable business. If the firm can identify what characteristics make those clients profitable, it will have a far clearer idea of the types of client that are attractive when analysing new business opportunities in the office catchment area. These characteristics are likely to include the client's turnover and profitability, range of services used, industry sector and entity type.

One way of doing this is to prepare a standard client information form for each client. Such forms will need to include details of any related clients, because the personal tax work for a director may, if seen in isolation, appear to be very unproductive. When viewed against the value of his company's work, however, the picture may be entirely different. The forms will also need to include the kind of client entity (i.e. whether a plc, limited company, partnership, sole trader, etc.), the industry sector in which it operates, and the value of each service used.

This exercise will be tedious and time-consuming, so as far as possible the completion of forms should be delegated to junior members of staff. However, the merits of the exercise will quickly become apparent as the completed forms highlight the profitability of each individual client to the firm, and the range of services used by that client. This in itself will identify opportunities for introducing additional services to the client.

Partners who provide specialist services in the firm should examine these forms to see on which clients they should concentrate their business development activities.

Clearly, this analysis is best undertaken by loading the information on to a computerised data base. If this can be fed from the time-recording system, so much the better: it then removes the need to update manually much of the information.

It is also important at this stage to analyse precisely where and how the firm's assignments originate, so that it can focus promotional activity on sources which can, or should, produce the most profitable work.

KEEPING TABS ON COMPETITORS

The days when potential clients simply turned up at the door are long past; accountants have to recognise that the profession is now intensely competitive, particularly in mature markets such as audit and tax compliance. Potential clients increasingly shop around to identify which firm can best meet their individual requirements. If a firm is to show such potential clients that its expertise and level of service are different to, and better than, those of competing firms, it needs to understand what its competitors are offering to clients.

To help build up an accurate picture, it may be useful to begin to build up files on each competitor, detailing services offered by them, the promotional techniques they use, the specific benefits they claim will accrue to clients using their services, and their fee rates and basis of charging. It is usually very difficult to ascertain this kind of information in more than anecdotal form; however, an awareness of the need to do this leads to an awareness of their offerings and sales messages, and the firm will gradually build a fairly comprehensive picture of their local business development strategies.

ESTABLISHING TARGET MARKETS

By undertaking the various activities suggested above, the firm will begin to limit the range of possible markets for its services. But before the firm can take the next step of defining the specific markets to focus on, it needs to determine, for each of its possible markets, what their particular needs are, and how well it can satisfy those needs relative to the competition, bearing in mind the limitations of its existing resources.

The factors likely to limit the amount of time and effort the firm devotes to marketing will include its current range of services; the extent to which it and its service range are known; the image clients and potential clients have of the firm and the quality of its services; its geographical location; its staff numbers and their level of experience, skills, and acceptability to clients; the quality of existing internal information and record-keeping systems; and the range and potential for further development of its existing client base. In some cases, because of the combination of these factors, the firm may decide that the particular groups which initially appeared to be an attractive proposition prove after analysis not to be so. This could apply as much to certain types of existing clients whom the firm has over the years continued to service, perhaps at the risk of diminishing margins, as to types of potential clients. The firm may also identify a number of high-risk clients who, while profitable, might be suddenly swept away by better-equipped competition, and therefore require increased attention.

Alternatively, the firm may decide that although it does not currently have the resources to cater competitively for the needs of a particular market, that market represents such attractive potential that resources to service it should be developed. Perhaps it needs to recruit specialist expertise or train existing staff for the job.

Having considered the various alternatives, the firm can then determine realistic goals for its marketing activities, so that it has targets to aim for, and against which to assess the progress of the firm. These might include:

- percentage increase in fees generated

- percentage increase in fees generated by specific services

- fees earned by partner or member of staff.

Whichever goals the firm decides to be appropriate, it must make sure that they are timed, measurable, and, above all, achievable. There is no point in setting unrealistic targets; as soon as partners and staff realise they are going to miss them, they will begin to question the point of the whole exercise and become demotivated.

Once the firm has specified the goals, it can then determine the major actions which will achieve them, i.e. its marketing strategy. This will start by defining its choice of the particular types of client it has decided to target. Then, for each of these markets, it might specify

- which existing services it wants to refine further or new services it wishes to develop, and the skill development required to provide the services
- how it will charge for the services, e.g. is there scope to charge on the value of the service to the client, rather than on the basis of the time it took?
- how it intends to differentiate them from the services offered by its competitors
- which benefits of using the firm it will stress in order to attract the target groups.

Having a marketing strategy is limiting: it recognises that the firm cannot do everything, and that it must give priority to certain specific directions. Once the firm has agreed these directions, it is in a strong position to concentrate its available resources on achieving the strategy, and it knows which alternative activities and opportunities to forgo.

HOW BEST TO ACCESS THE CHOSEN MARKETS

Existing clients

The existing client base will inevitably form the primary market: to ignore this is as effective as pouring water into a bath with no plug. Thus, the firm's overriding priority will be to safeguard and increase the profitability to it of its existing clients. The most effective way of doing this is to treat existing clients in the same way as any other market and to develop a timed, co-ordinated activity plan to be implemented by individual assignment partners.

Various techniques and practices to achieve this goal are at your disposal.

The firm might, for example, modify the engagement letter so that it emphasises the level and quality of service the client will receive, the frequency with which the assignment leader will report on progress, and the close working relationship between the firm's staff and the client's staff that the firm will attempt to generate. Partners might 'add value' by discussing with the client at the end of assignments any areas which their professional experience suggests could be improved or strengthened. Two of the largest accounting firms have already spent substantial amounts of money advertising the fact that they do this. This type of review session opens up new selling opportunities in that the firm may be able to introduce additional services to rectify weaknesses identified. However, it needs to be handled with discretion, because the client may feel that his operations are being criticised.

Two further techniques are simply good client relations. The first is to remain in touch between assignments, to remove any impression that the firm is interested in the client's welfare only when it is earning fees. The second is to maintain notes of personal details of the client, hopes and intentions for future development, matters he has discussed regarding what is happening within his industry, etc. A record of the press reports on competition and the industry itself should be kept. Clients expect their advisers to understand their operations and their industry fully, and an accountant's credibility will be enhanced if he can refer in conversation to current developments and discuss their likely implications. The exercise will be of additional value when it is necessary to introduce new staff members to the assignment team: such notes will help them to get up to scratch in the shortest time.

Introducers

The analysis of how past work has been generated, referred to earlier, will give the firm a better idea of which individuals and firms have been the most productive referral sources in the past. These are likely to include satisfied existing clients, and their bankers and solicitors with whom the firm may have worked. Other bankers and solicitors may on occasion refer clients who need the services of a trusted accountant. Partners and staff members may identify opportunities through their social contacts.

Seminars run by the firm, and advertisements and entries placed by it in directories, may result in further leads.

It was suggested above that the firm concentrate its activities on the sources which either have been, or it feels should be, most productive. If records have not been kept in the past to show where new work has come from and how it was generated, the firm needs to establish such systems and make sure accurate records are maintained. It can then formulate 'mini-marketing plans' for each productive referral source. These might include letting clients know that the firm will welcome work referred by them, and obtain their permission to use them as references if required. Specify the type of work most attractive to the firm, otherwise it may receive a stream of introductions of low-quality, unprofitable work which it turns down at the risk of its relationship with the client.

New clients

The remaining 'markets' for the firm's services are those individuals, firms and companies who are potential users of its services, or of services it could develop if required. But the firm may decide that the categories already considered constitute sufficient business, or at least as much business as it feels able to service. Certainly, it would be detrimental to take on additional work and thereby cause the service to existing clients to suffer.

However, if the firm has carried out the analysis suggested above, it is likely it will have identified clients who are unprofitable, unlikely to become profitable, and who do not need to be retained because of their connection to other profitable clients. Therefore the capacity to service new work exists.

If the firm does wish to identify and attract potential clients, it will need to develop some form of prospecting process, so that the activities of those involved can be effectively directed. The following is a suggested approach.

First, define the catchment area of the practice, i.e. the area it is practical for partners and staff to service. Second, use the conclusions from the earlier analysis to define the types of potential client the firm most wishes to attract, either because of their likely profitability (now or at a defined future stage of their development), their prestige value to the firm (in terms of attracting and retaining staff, the credibility they bestow on the firm, etc.), or their strategic value (their value as evidence of the firm's ability to handle specific types of work).

The firm can then identify such potential clients by using, for example, local knowledge, local trade and business directories, Yellow Pages, Thomson local directories, etc. Once the firm has identified individuals or organisations to approach, it should list them in the order of their attractiveness, bearing in mind it will be able to service only a proportion of those whose business has been identified as desirable.

PROMOTIONAL ACTIVITIES TO ATTRACT NEW CLIENTS

It is only when the firm has defined its marketing goals and strategies that it can determine:

- the particular sales message to direct at each target group, matching only the relevant benefits and relevant services to their specific needs

- the most appropriate promotional techniques to use

- the resources required to ensure the success of the promotional techniques and activities chosen

- the procedures to introduce to review individual techniques or activities so that they can be further refined for future use.

Many firms fall into the trap of trying to promote themselves generally, to 'increase name awareness'. There is some limited merit in this, in that it may make potential clients more receptive to a later approach from the firm. However, any message that the recipients see to be of direct relevance to their specific needs is bound to have greater impact – hence the constant requirement to understand what these likely needs are.

The best way to establish the needs of a target group is to 'brainstorm' with a group of experienced partners and managers who know similar clients or organisations. The firm can then attempt to list these needs in order of their likely priority, and develop a 'sales message' which explicitly links the benefits its service can deliver to those priority needs.

When the firm has determined what it wants to say to specific groups, it must choose the media to relay that message.

Marketing in practice for accountants

A wide range of promotional activities and techniques is now available to accountants, including coverage on TV and radio, press relations, sponsorship, advertising, direct mail, exhibitions, seminars, talks to professional bodies, newsletters, promotional booklets, and the use of promotional items (see Chapter 8). With so wide a range of techniques available, as well as being bombarded with suggestions from advertisers who wish to relieve the firm of large chunks of its promotional budget, it can be difficult to decide which, if any, to use.

It helps to remember that, no matter how effective the firm's promotional activities may be, they alone cannot produce clients. It is only through face-to-face selling that initial interest, generated by successful promotional activities, can be converted into actual business.

If partners and staff lack the necessary skills to generate additional business from existing clients, communicate effectively with introducers, and persuade potential clients of the benefits of using the firm's services in preference to those of its competitors, time and money spent on other promotional activities are wasted. It is therefore sensible to concentrate initially on developing partner and staff sales and presentation skills, and only then consider the additional techniques available.

Skill development

If accountants are to make a success of promotional activities they are likely to need a range of knowledge and skills which may be new to them.

First, they will require a knowledge of services available from the firm, symptoms in the clients' operations which indicate a need for these services, and the benefits which such services provide. These can be imparted through written notes, or preferably by internal seminars run by the firm's specialists and backed up by summary notes and checklists.

Second, accountants will need skills in taking a brief from a new client, and presenting the benefits of the relevant services to meet the needs identified. Written notes and training films can increase staff understanding of good practice, but true skill development will be achieved only by pooling actual experience with individual tutoring, ideally by means of closed-circuit television playback. People learn best from making their own mistakes and then agreeing, with a sympathetic expert, ways of rectifying such mistakes.

Third, as they become more senior, accountants will need to develop skills in preparing written proposals and presenting such proposals to potential clients. (The same presentation skills will be required if the firm decides to run seminars or speak to local professional groups.) Again, written guidelines can minimise the time it takes to prepare proposals and presentations, but skill development requires the same tutoring as for selling skills above.

Smaller firms are unlikely to have individuals skilled in business development training on their staff, and may need to use external training resources. If this is the case, the best option is likely to be to commission a specific training programme for several members of staff at a time, rather than send individuals to outside, general courses. The effectiveness of such training will depend on the trainers' understanding of the firm and the range of situations in which the skills will be used, so it is important to spend time thoroughly briefing them (see Chapter 3).

Once these skills are in place – or, more realistically, at the same time as these skills are being developed – which other techniques should the firm contemplate? The following comments are in line with the approach suggested above, that the firm should concentrate its efforts on the techniques likely to have the greatest initial impact. The following techniques have the additional attraction that they can be fairly closely monitored and their success gauged.

Prepare some form of promotional booklet

When partners or staff are establishing relations with introducers and talking to potential clients, it helps to have some written material which provides evidence of the firm's capabilities. This does not need to be glossy or highly developed, but should include a brief description of the firm, the services available, and the quality and experience of partners and staff. Emphasis throughout the text should be on what the service will actually achieve for the client, not on details of the service itself.

Consider running client seminars

A well-organised seminar which incorporates well-prepared, proficient speakers can bestow great credibility on the firm. Assuming that the subject matter is of interest and value to the chosen audience, it will demonstrate the firm's competence in that subject. If there is a coffee break and, say, wine and snacks to follow, partners and staff have the opportunity to speak to those attending to generate possible business. Invitations sent out are in fact well-targeted advertisements, and the event may receive coverage in the local press.

Such seminars do, however, take considerable organisation and demand substantial allocation of time by both administrators and speakers. If they are to succeed, it will be necessary to:

1 Clarify the objectives beforehand, and share those objectives with all concerned.
2 Set quantified targets, be they fees generated, contacts made, or whatever, so that there is a yardstick against which to measure the success of the event.
3 Set a budget appropriate to the objectives for the event.
4 Pool reactions to the success of the event immediately afterwards, agree ways in which future events could be improved, and specify who should be responsible for follow-up activities.
5 Fix a review date for, say, three months later, to review whether any increase in business has resulted.

All too often post-seminar activities are ignored, with the result that leads are not developed and opportunities are missed.

Press coverage

Perhaps the best way to illustrate the value to a firm of editorial press coverage is by comparing it with advertising. In advertising the advertiser pays for a space and (within certain constraints) can choose what to say within that space. However, people recognise the advertised message for what it is: a partisan, rosy picture of a service or of a firm, showing only one, biased, side of the picture. They therefore take the message with a large pinch of salt, if they read it at all. The second major drawback is of course the cost of advertising.

This is not to say that a firm should ignore all advertising: it will continue to be a technique which can be used to great effect in recruitment, to publicise the firm as part of a specific campaign, to support a seminar, or to introduce a new service.

The great advantage of editorial coverage in the press, on the other hand, is that it bestows credibility on what is being said, simply because a piece has been written by a supposedly neutral third party. The cost of obtaining that coverage is the time it takes to establish a relationship with editors and journalists, and to keep them informed of news. This might involve an occasional lunch with journalists, preparation of press releases, and responding to journalists' enquiries.

There are, however, risks in dealing with the press. The first is that journalists very rarely print a story exactly as the firm would like it: they are not interested in what goes on within the firm unless they can identify an angle which will be of interest to their readers. Once the firm has given them the information, it cannot retain full control over the eventual result. It is possible to go a long way to maintaining some control, by supplying factual written material, by being careful in how comments are phrased, and by communicating only with representatives of reputable publications. The firm may find, however, that when the piece is published, the tone and emphasis is rather different from what it had intended!

As to the remaining promotional techniques available, experience in developing those already mentioned will establish the habit of considering the needs of the people the firm is trying to influence, and the time and money the firm wishes to devote to attracting their business. If the firm applies these criteria to future situations which arise, it can determine which of the available methods, or which combination, to bring to bear to achieve its specific objectives.

THE VALUE OF OUTSIDE ASSISTANCE

A firm is unlikely to have the expertise among its partners and staff to implement all the projects and techniques described above, and so it may wish to enlist the occasional help of outside specialists. These might include

- strategic marketing consultants, to help review current activities and advise on possible business development strategies

- professional trainers, to develop partner and staff skills in prospecting, face-to-face selling and presentation
- designers, to put together promotional material and, where necessary, advertisements
- public relations advisers, to help establish and maintain a relationship with the local press, or for their help in setting up and running specific events.

If a firm does utilise the services of any of these experts, it should clarify beforehand what it wishes to achieve from the exercise and give them as specific and comprehensive a brief as possible. This will enable them to understand the firm's priorities from the outset. It can of course assume that they will recommend additional areas for consideration, which can then be assessed against these objectives.

The firm should ensure that the experts' initial proposals include frequent review stages. This will enable it to have the assurance that they are achieving the agreed goals, which means that any further stages will be justified and explained before they are undertaken (see Chapter 9).

If the firm is training its staff, it may wish to put partners through the training first so that staff recognise the importance of the time invested. Partners will also thereby have a fuller understanding of the techniques their teams are acquiring, and be more likely to ensure these newly developed skills are fully used.

IN CONCLUSION

This chapter has outlined a framework to help a firm develop its practice by applying the range of activities which fall under the banner of 'marketing'. The actions suggested are realistic in that they have all been applied successfully. Those who decide to use some or all of these suggestions will find the process at times perhaps frustrating, but ultimately rewarding.

To those who remain unconvinced of the need for marketing in the accounting profession, a word of warning is appropriate. Users of accounting services are more prone nowadays to review their existing advisers periodically. New clients have become more sophisticated, and shop around. More and more competitors employ effective marketing techniques.

The result? If a firm does not employ such techniques, it runs the risk of providing clients with services they no longer want or need. They may replace those services with those that they perceive to be more appropriate – even if in reality they are the same as what they already receive.

New clients may exclude a firm from their list of possible suppliers, simply because it has not made them aware of what it has to offer. By not taking action, that firm may be overtaken.

Each firm must choose.

13

MARKETING IN PRACTICE FOR SOLICITORS
by Robert Hall

EDITORS' PREVIEW

Robert Hall, a solicitor, is a partner in the London office of Baker and McKenzie. He is currently engaged in the property department.

Baker and McKenzie is the largest law firm in the world, with over 470 partners and more than 1,400 lawyers of many nationalities operating from nearly fifty offices in the major financial and commercial centres of Europe, the Middle East, North and South America, Australia and the Pacific Basin.

In this chapter Robert Hall lays great stress on the need to analyse and understand the true nature of a solicitor's 'product' before even attempting to develop a marketing strategy. Just producing a range of glossy pamphlets describing services is not in itself the answer, because the essential element of 'differentiation' can be missed.

WHAT IS MEANT BY 'MARKETING FOR SOLICITORS'

The earlier chapters in this book have identified, analysed and exhaustively described the subject of marketing, its planning and its application. They have provided a comprehensive blueprint for progress in one of the more nebulous yet central areas in which a service business, if it is to survive, must be successful. Such a business may prosper and grow largely through luck, but growth which is successful and rewarding will mostly only be achieved if it is planned.

The first ten chapters of this book, which describe how to achieve that success, may have left the reader with the impression that the mere following of the processes already described will be all that is necessary in order to achieve a successful result. If only it were that simple. The learning of a technique does not mean that it can be practised. A brilliant academic with much depth of learning cannot necessarily teach.

So it is with marketing for solicitors. The theory is fine. The reader will applaud the well-thought-out and presented proposals. Aspects of the blueprint will be recognised as not unlike tentative promotional efforts already attempted. An encouraging similarity with the reality of a solicitor's practice can sometimes be found. However, a nagging concern will have troubled the solicitor/reader: 'The principle is fine; the results must be good; I am persuaded that marketing is "a good thing". But how is it to be applied to a solicitor's practice; is it possible – or perhaps even desirable – that solicitors' work, my product, my firm's product, should be packaged, presented, exploited, marketed?'

These are fundamental questions, and of such profound seriousness that they should not be scorned or minimised. They lead to a consideration of two basic preliminary questions which must be understood before a firm of solicitors can properly undertake marketing: 'What is meant by marketing for solicitors?' and 'What is it that a solicitor should be marketing?'

Marketing is defined earlier in this book as 'the management process responsible for identifying, anticipating and satisfying customer requirements profitably'. That is admirable as a statement of principle and as a management objective. It is the process of achieving that result which often remains concealed in secrecy. The 4-minute mile is a fine target. How do you achieve it?

Every practising lawyer would like to think that he or she has the confidence to achieve planned objectives. In that respect we would no doubt hope to be regarded in the same way as that somewhat rare breed – the law firm that is cohesively committed to a co-operatively analysed and constructed medium- and long-term development strategy, and which in addition has the ability while implementing that strategy to assess and modify it without losing sight of the key objectives. The important point here, however, is that just as such a well-organised firm will have as one of its foundations strong self-esteem, so it is necessary that each individual's self-perception should be manifested in confidence in him or herself.

Inevitably, perhaps, we all like to think well of ourselves, because that is how we hope others think of us. It is, however, a most important prerequisite to successful practice. Indeed the mere act of offering services for hire implies a degree of the self-confidence which is required. It is in any event a good and essential base from which to start. The collective self-esteem of a firm is the aggregate of each individual's confidence in himself or herself and in what he or she is doing. This individual and corporate self-confidence will in turn help to establish another fundamentally important requirement for the successful practice of law, namely a belief in the product. And that, of course, is *the* basic marketing rule.

Assuming that the appropriate degree of self-belief is attained, we need in addition to have at least a sufficiency of the other capabilities – 'skills' is the current jargon word – which will enable us to turn that self-belief into making a living in an interesting, varied and fulfilling way. Therefore we have views and approaches on matters such as management of time, management of staff, professional development, provision of property from which to practice, handling of increasingly complex data systems, development of the practice, finding new business, recruitment – in other words 'management' in its multi-faceted breadth. Indeed the many aspects of 'management' could so crowd into the day that it may seem that there is little time left to do what one is after all trained to do, namely the practice of law. However, the purpose of marketing, properly applied, is not to create further burdens, but to give purpose and direction to the continuous effort which must be made to identify, anticipate and satisfy client requirements. That effort, however, will not be made in the isolation of a vacuum. As with all other businesses, a solicitor's practice must take account of the world as it is.

A CHANGING ENVIRONMENT

It is truism to say that our world is changing rapidly. Significant economic changes are taking place. There are revolutionary developments in office equipment. This is particularly and brutally true in regard to the speed with which the fundamental building block of our professional life – the written word – can be drafted, redrafted, agreed, disputed, resolved, recorded, transmitted and finally logged for posterity. Furthermore there are some fundamental revolutionary forces blowing in the outside world which question the very basis upon which the legal profession in this country is organised, its method of control and self-regulation and the system of provision of legal services. The issue of merger between the two branches of the legal profession will not diminish, and indeed it seems inevitable that merger will take place.

The 1992 European 'big bang' may not seem quite so dramatic in fact, but the pressure for change will continue, with other European qualified lawyers being able to hang their shingle anywhere in the EEC. The present taste against monopolies will prevail, and issues of regulation of standards, whether by the profession or the state, will ensure that our profession continues to attract critical attention. All of this is entirely proper. Indeed there is nothing much worse than moribund self-satisfaction.

Nevertheless it is in this context of change that we have to prepare if we are to avoid being trapped in the past. A firm which does not so prepare may be lucky and survive happily, but it could equally suffer a serious reverse and become aimless, disenchanted and prone to self-doubt. That is not an appropriate condition in which it is likely to be of much use to its clients.

THE NEED TO PLAN

A firm needs to know in what direction it is headed. In addition it needs to know in what direction it would like to be going. Those desired objectives need to have been tested realistically against what it can at present offer or expect in the future to be able to offer to its clients. In other words, a plan is required – a plan which defines practice objectives, realistically and achievably, in a time-related context, and the strategies for achieving those objectives. Based on that, it is then possible to develop budgets, staff forecasts, space requirements – the whole host of good business decisions which will provide the administrative framework within which the practice can develop with purpose and confidence.

Without a plan there will be no real need for marketing, because there will be no business achievement target to promote and therefore attain. Equally, marketing without a plan will be largely futile, since it is unlikely that the firm will know what is selling or why. Marketing in such circumstances will be a potentially expensive exercise in self-delusion: an effort giving the appearance of action, but which in reality is confusing and damaging.

'Marketing' is not a new concept. In one shape or form it has been with businesses and professions for many years. We should not think therefore that marketing is the creation of the 'adman' or the business development consultant. The fact that such an area of activity, and particularly marketing for solicitors, has become identified by such experts and is being exploited by them as an activity in its own right is a measure of the degree to which solicitors have failed to deal with the topic adequately themselves. That is certainly a criticism, but not a damning one. It is a measure of the extent to which the practice of law, in the full breath of the meaning of that phrase, has become more and more complicated. Law is not in that respect materially different from other activities. Business in general has become more complex, more diffuse, more competitive, more subject to the pressure of unexpected influences. Therefore, like any other business, a solicitor's practice needs to spend more time anticipating the unexpected so as to be able to cope with the competition.

In other words, it is essential to get down to some really basic questions about what we do. We practise in an increasingly complex and client-demand-led environment. The days when a solicitor simply waited for people, reaching certain stages of their lives, inevitably to call for his services are now all but gone. Property transactions can be carried out by licensed conveyancers; grants of probate and administration of estates are dealt with by banks; tax planning is offered by accountants; financial and business advice is increasingly provided by merchant banks. The prospective client therefore has a range of options from which to select when deciding how to deal with any particular problem that arises. We live in an increasingly competitive environment which will become more so and in which we are increasingly not the first choice for advice. About that point we must be totally frank with ourselves.

Solicitors have no option but to compete in the market-place. They must identify, anticipate and satisfy client requirements, and seek to do that profitably.

DEVELOPING THE COMPETITIVE STRATEGY

In order to compete it is necessary to have a strategy, which in turn can only be developed if there is a clear understanding both of one's own firm and of the competitors in the chosen area of practice. Consideration of those issues raises fundamental questions about the whole business of the practice of law. What firm are we now? What sort of firm do we wish to be? In what field do we wish to compete? What realistically could we expect to be able to offer and within what period of time? What other firms or service providers (e.g. banks, accountants) are competing in our present and preferred future fields? If we set in train a programme of expansion and practice development, will we at the end of that period of development have the desire to manage the increased practice (which will almost inevitably mean more staff, more space, more clients, more complex regulatory issues, etc.)? Will the plans we are at present formulating be appropriate to the practice as it will be at the end of the presently proposed lifetime of the plan currently being contemplated? Will the new partners be likely to agree to what the present partners are proposing? Perhaps even more fundamentally, are we certain that law will in fact at the end of the lifetime of the projected plan be practised in the same manner as it is now, i.e. will a partnership co-operating in the same way as at present still be relevant, or will the merging of solicitors and barristers, and perhaps other professions, require a completely different method of organisation? Will the advent of professional corporations combined with tax treatment militate against ever-growing practices? Will the coming of increasingly greater electronic sophistication mean that the congregation of so many qualified lawyers under one roof with the relevant number of support staff amounts to no more than an ancient tribal custom totally unsuited to the brave new data-chip-controlled world?

Thus it is that seriously addressing questions arising in connection with marketing for solicitors raises fundamental issues about the practice of law. We have in effect to be prepared to spend time agreeing on a set of aims and objectives which are not too vague or generalised but are coherent and constructive and are reasonably achievable within the time span of the proposed plan.

It cannot be emphasised too strongly that, when preparing to launch into the marketing whirl, it is essential to assess or reassess or consider for the first time corporately and co-operatively, such fundamental aspects, the honest review of which will produce a firm basis upon which to build future plans. The failure to do so can have results which are almost too obvious to point out.

INVOLVING THE MANAGEMENT TEAM

A further central and essential requirement of such a review is that it should involve all of the members of the partnership, who should be urged to contribute their time and thought to the review. The benefits of such involvement are again obvious, but nevertheless worth mentioning. The first benefit, somewhat negative, is that no one can complain at a later stage that they were not consulted. There have been some dramatic recent examples of fundamental arrangements being made for partnerships without proper consultation, in consequence of which such partnerships have disintegrated. Such a result could hardly be said to be a triumph of strategic planning. The second benefit is positive, namely that a plan co-operatively produced, discussed and agreed upon is a better plan for that reason, and it will accordingly attract greater loyalty and support, and therefore have a greater chance of success. There is nothing so sapping to an individual, or so likely to lead to the self-doubt that is inimical to the practice of law, than the knowledge or suspicion of a self-appointed cabal disposing of the future over the heads of others.

The plan therefore must be co-operatively analysed and developed. Clearly it is appropriate that a group of individual partners be allocated specific responsibility for collating the relevant data to provide the core information on which to propose a plan for consideration by the partnership as a whole. Such partners should be reasonably representative of the partnership, both in terms of practice areas and, for example, age profile. The establishment of such a representative committee should again have the benefit of investing the outline proposals it produces with some chance of preliminary broad-based confidence.

Once such self-assessment has been completed, the partnership will be in a position to determine when and where to compete. Existing and developing resources can be targeted to achieve the chosen strategic objective. The prospects of success will be significantly increased if either the required resources are available or, in anticipation, the necessary preparations to provide those resources have been made.

The process of marketing is the marshalling of those resources in such a fashion as, while meeting the requirements of the target (i.e. the client group), attains the strategic objective and profitably satisfies the participants (i.e. the partners) in the campaign. In other words, it is more than just 'selling', or targeting effort, or providing the chosen service. It is the entire process of identifying the target (the needs of the potential client which are to be satisfied), preparing for development of the target (planning the campaign), battling successfully to capture and satisfy the target (providing the correct resources when and where they are required) and winning (achieving the objective profitably and retaining the target). It is the whole process of competition: defining, planning, doing, winning.

WHAT SHOULD A SOLICITOR BE MARKETING?

It is important to know what is being marketed, since different aspects of the product require different treatment in the competitive process. Furthermore an analysis of the product will help to deepen understanding about one's firm. It will thereby provide a broader base of knowledge and will accordingly strengthen the process of determining how to attain the chosen strategic objective.

What a solicitor sells is his skill at interpreting the law in the service of or in relation to the client's stated objective. It is the application of the law rather than the mere recital of it. It is the act of construing it, negotiating a contract, being an advocate of a particular view. That is what the client, the customer, requires and pays for. The skill is provided either orally (as in advocacy and negotiation) or in writing (preparation of documents). The basic unit of such provision is the word.

Thus the solicitor's product which is to be marketed, i.e. used in a particular planned way in order to achieve the strategic objective, is his skill in interpreting the law. It is not as such the oral or written word, although that is the medium through which the product is provided. If the product was the word alone, it could simply be provided by mechanical data bases, as indeed it is now. There are extensive libraries at the behest of a button, huge reservoirs of accumulated knowledge, great texts of case law, all available on the asking of the right question or the selection of the appropriate key word or phrase. And yet the solicitor is the interpreter of that great accumulation. Acting as such an interpreter requires knowledge, judgement, presentation. It is in fact quite a creative process. It is that which the solicitor sells.

In this context it is important to realise that the mere written or spoken word is not enough. Frequently reference is made to 'the work product', as if that were 'the be-all and end-all' of the solicitor's function. It is represented as if it were his product – his sole purpose. We would, however, be seriously misleading ourselves if we were to think that that is the product which is to be marketed. That leads to the conclusion that marketing is solely about words, or the glossiest distribution of written material. Hence great emphasis is placed on learned treatises on this or that subject, topical issues, news magazines, distributions with portentous titles. Sometimes such items are well presented with a clear, recognisable 'house style'; sometimes they are embarrassingly bad. In the end, however, all they are is written work product, items which can be produced by more or less anyone who cares to spend the time and effort.

This is not to decry the value of written work product with a coherent and consistent house style. Dividends can certainly be gained by the judicious use of such materials. But yielding to the temptation to regard the sole function of marketing as being the production and distribution of written work product can easily result in solicitors becoming little more than publishing houses, measuring success mainly by reference to the number of pamphlets produced.

The consequence of that view is that the development and polishing of the solicitor's real skill and purpose is left to chance. It means that the marketing effort will be misdirected, concentrating solely or mainly on pamphlet production rather than geared towards demonstrating why it is that your firm has the particular skills required by the chosen target customer. It further means that the essential effort required to develop those skills (for example, training in public speaking, negotiating, drafting) may often not be made. In other words, the wrong thing – the written product – will have been marketed, rather than the person who has the skills of interpretation. In short, the consequence of misunderstanding the nature of the solicitor's product is that the strategies chosen to market that solicitor's practice could well be wrong. This in turn could result in disillusionment and frustration – a recipe for anguish and self-doubt.

OTHER MATTERS

There are four further matters it is appropriate to consider briefly at this point – the provision of resources, review machinery, the need to market, and constraints.

The provision of resources

Having struggled and debated to produce a plan and the strategies to be employed in order to achieve the marketing objectives, the partners must ensure that the right resources are not only at present available, but will be provided in the course of the plan to meet the expected demand. The nature of the resources required will plainly depend upon the type of practice and the areas into which expansion is proposed. Thus it is important, once the plan is laid down, to tailor present and future resources to it.

Recruitment programmes must be geared up and paced according to the firm's needs (and that in turn opens up for review and arrangement the whole area of recruitment, organisation of interviews, training for interviews, instituting 'exit polling' to ascertain reasons for rejection of job offers). Space provision must be organised adequately and in good time to ensure that the working environment is maintained and improved. If that is not done, staff may move because better facilities are offered elsewhere – a situation which cannot really be afforded in view of the investment that will have been made in that individual's skills, and a result which in any event could not be said to result from successful strategic planning.

In particular, however, the personal skills of existing and future staff must be developed. Programmes must be established for improving skills in public speaking, negotiating, drafting. Effort and thought must be directed in this way so that the product – the interpreting of the law – is improved. The benefit, apart from the obvious one of giving better value for money to the client, is that it will contribute substantially to improvement in each individual's self-esteem, and thereby indirectly to morale in the firm.

As will be clear, these are all aspects of marketing, none of which should be regarded as a luxury. Continuing professional development, in the sense of keeping up to date with developments in the law, is of course essential. That is part of the product as well. However, the additional aspects described above will meet the definition of those parts of marketing which constitute 'anticipating and satisfying customer requirements'.

Review machinery

Every plan is based upon assumptions as to future events. The achievement of the plan's objective will be dependent upon certain results occurring in consequence of the putting into effect of the steps of the plan.

There is of course nothing surprising in this. However, the future has always been uncertain, and will remain so. So we have to accept that that is the context in which the plan is to function.

So far as is known there are only three ways to approach the future. The first is to make no serious preparation at all, but simply trust to instinct and luck. In business terms that is not regarded as being constructive or sensible. The second is to try and control the future. From a business point of view that means that if you can control the supply, you can thereby control the manner in which the demand is satisfied; or rather you supply what you want instead of what the public may want. In product terms this means market domination – a monopoly. Unfortunately this approach to the control of the future is not permitted. Monopoly is out. The third approach to the future is really that which has been painstakingly outlined in this book. So far as is reasonably possible you need to make an assessment of your future by considering your past and your present, and your likely resources; predictions are made as to future events, thereby enabling you to make reasonable, even though cautious, assumptions in order to provide the framework within which your plan is established. That is a rational way in which to proceed.

Such a plan is, however, still subject to the vagaries of future events, or simply to failure to take certain steps or implement certain arrangements as planned. To know whether this is happening, it goes without saying that it is essential to have a mechanism or a review system in place to monitor the plan as it is implemented *and* take any corrective action. Failure to monitor will of course mean that it will not be known whether corrective action is required. Furthermore failure to have agreed upon and have in existence an effective system which can, as required, implement corrective action would be foolish. Why have a plan if there is no means of ensuring that it is adhered to or corrected when it is found to have made some erroneous assumptions as to the future?

Again, this may seem such an obvious point. Yet the inertia of any bureaucracy should not be underestimated, both in terms of what it has been directed to do and what it does in fact do. By way of illustration consider recent examples of major defence contracts undertaken by governmental organisations where significant cost overruns have arisen. When investigated, these were found to have been due simply to management failure to review the programme and take corrective action.

The success of a plan depends not only upon its devising and its execution, but also upon the review and control of its implementation. That is common sense.

The need to market

The purpose of this book is to demonstrate how, and why, the product of a lawyer, or an accountant, or the provider of financial services can be marketed. It may be thought that it is implied that there is really no need to spend time discussing whether or not to market, since the objective evidence inevitably leads to the conclusion 'market or die'. Though there may be some merit in that shotgun approach, it is, however, important to accept that a decision to market *is* a personal one, and one which can only validly be reached after careful consideration of properly evaluated aims and objectives.

Nevertheless, even though each firm must make its own personal assessment on whether it wishes to market itself, and if so how, there are aspects which arise in any consideration of whether to market which are capable of evaluation from an objective point of view. Thus, for example, it can be conclusively demonstrated that market-share improvement or development into new market areas will follow the implementation of certain actions, or again it will be incontrovertible that failure and disappointment will result from not providing adequate resources to deal with increased demand.

There are, however, other factors, less verifiable but nevertheless real, which should be considered. As has already been said, the business and professional environment in which a lawyer functions is at present subject to dramatic and increasingly urgent pressures, which suggest as a likely consequence fundamental changes in working practices. The development of new machinery and communications systems, which has speeded up many processes which previously proved laborious and trying, can justify examining how to improve legal services. The likelihood of a fused profession and possibly multi-disciplinary practices must mean that it is at least sensible to consider very seriously how such realities should be dealt with and what preparations should be made.

While those are in a sense personal decisions, the essential point is that even in those respects which do not call for consideration of whether to extend existing practice areas or to develop new ones, external and foreseeable events *will* mean that changes must be made in practice. Other firms will expand and develop, and will compete. It is this contributor's view that it is essential to have a plan for the future and that marketing (in the sense described in this book) is an essential part of successful firm management.

Constraints

It is not the purpose of this chapter to set out a handbook of 'dos and dont's' in marketing for lawyers, nor is it intended to describe the regulatory frameworks or practice guidelines stipulated by statute and the Law Society. Other texts do that with great clarity. Nevertheless it is appropriate to point out that there are a number of constraints which any firm of solicitors must bear in mind. Our regulatory authority, the Law Society, is statutorily obliged to stipulate standards in our professional conduct, and it of course does so. It may perhaps sometimes be thought that this duty is discharged in a somewhat straitlaced manner. Nevertheless it is most important that the rules on advertising (as from time to time modified) be observed carefully, since there is little point in having a marketing plan which leads to censure and suspension. You cannot by law provide the service you seek to promote if, to put it bluntly, you do not have your practising certificate.

The requirements set by the Law Society, if followed, should ensure that the standards of advertising authorities are complied with. Judgement and care will also be required as to the tone and style of any advertising undertaken.

CONCLUSIONS

Although it is true that marketing is a virtually inevitable requirement of modern management of a legal practice, the decision on whether or not to market is a personal one. It is not just that each individual firm must determine its own tone, pace and style in any marketing campaign it undertakes. Such a campaign in addition needs committed support from each individual in the partnership. *You* need to want to market; *you* need to be prepared to support difficult decisions which will inevitably arise during the course of implementation of the plan. *You* may need to ask yourself the question 'Do we have the will and determination to succeed?' It is to be hoped so.

14

MARKETING IN PRACTICE FOR FINANCIAL SERVICES

by Kevin Gavaghan

EDITORS' PREVIEW

Kevin Gavaghan is the marketing director of Midland Bank Plc, and as such has been at the forefront of the fast-developing use of strategic marketing in the financial services sector.

As Kevin Gavaghan points out, marketing financial services is the most advanced form of marketing among all professional services today, which makes this chapter a most appropriate final demonstration of marketing in practice.

MARKETING FINANCIAL SERVICES

Marketing financial services is the most advanced form of marketing among professional services; for banks, building societies and insurance companies operate in mass markets and spend considerable sums on professional and systematic product development and communications. Given the level of expenditure, it is not surprising that techniques used by companies selling fast-moving consumer goods have had their early applications in financial services. Those applications vary widely.

Few organisations have structured their marketing departments on the lines of those in FMCG companies where research and analysis lead to product development and communications in a way designed to encourage systematic fulfilment of market needs almost on a production-line basis. There is still a tendency to believe that financial industries are different from others and that financial products and services have to have a bespoke element to them.

This chapter sets out to establish that, with the appropriate organisation, resources and business decision structure, successful new product development and implementation is achieved as a matter of course. Law and accounting firms will follow where financial organisations have led, and the emphasis will be on successful business-to-business marketing.

Three case histories demonstrate the steps

This chapter describes three campaigns where the techniques of consumer goods marketing have been deployed with clear objectives against precisely targeted groups. The first case history is a straightforward example of target marketing, simple packaging and appropriate communication. The second case history describes a campaign to increase market share and profitability and to maximise cross sales to the new customer base, over a 3-year period. A third case history sets out the research and analysis which led to the repackaging of a product aimed at the business start-up market. A service which had been on offer from a bank for 2 years was revitalised, sales took off and the bank's image with this target group was raised measurably.

The three case histories are set out after a brief appreciation of the market conditions prevailing at the time of launch and an analysis of the major forces for change in the financial services environment.

Five essential steps to successful marketing

Marketing financial services is different to marketing other goods and services in only one way. It has to be done with greater precision, care and understanding, because its basis generally is a long-term relationship with a customer, and that relationship is concerned with money. Viewed through the eyes of the purveyor, the principles of marketing are constant:

Identify the desired customer base.

Determine the specific needs of the targeted customer group(s).

Produce products and services that (a) meet those needs, (b) make profits, and (c) differentiate.

Communicate and deliver the products or services to the market.

Commit the sales force.

The customer's perspective is even more simple: 'Recognise me as an individual. Meet my needs in ways which work, are reliable, accessible, convenient and at a price I will pay.' Increasingly he or she will demand that the products and services are rendered in a style or manner which fits the customer's own self-perception. This will range from basic and no frills to stylish, elegant, practical or packaged.

Expressed in this way, the principles of marketing look straightforward and the customers' requirements elementary. But the complexity of markets and speed of change, together with the often out-of-date and inappropriate organisational structures of many suppliers, make a miss as likely as a hit. Today the cost of money, manpower and materials deployed in pursuit of the customers' business makes misses expensive. The Latin and Anglo-Saxon origins of profit and loss, *profectus* meaning advance and *los* meaning destruction, are never more relevant than in financial services marketing today.

A new bank, building society or insurance company applying to its bank manager or its merchant bank for a loan to start a business today would not pass the first hurdle without a good business plan. The business plan would be in two parts, namely marketing and financial; its scope would include markets, products and services, promotion, people, premises, delivery, systems, information and profit.

THE MARKETING PENTAGRAM

In financial services traditionally there have been two major categories of organisation: those which are primarily 'manufacturers' of products and services, such as the insurance and investment funds companies; and others which are largely 'distributors', such as the High-Street banks and building societies. As competition and deregulation have lowered barriers, each major category has sought to extend and improve the scope and quality of its onslaught on the market – in the one case by looking for new methods and outlets for distribution and in the other by extending the range of products it sells. In the process each has become concerned with the complete chain of activities which comprise marketing:

- Products
- Premises
- People
- Processes
- Positioning

Cumulative effect of five Ps

In an increasingly competitive environment where there has historically been little differentiation, it is unlikely that any company contending for the customer's business will break away from the pack and establish a huge lead or a major and permanent difference between itself and its challengers. Woody Allen, commenting on business, once said, 'Competitive advantage is being 15 minutes ahead – all the time!' The reality is that large and medium companies will only really succeed in terms of customer loyalty and profit if they can establish service standards and performance levels that are '15 minutes ahead' on each of the key items on the list of Ps. The cumulative impact of a modest lead in each – product features, premises design and function, people service, computer or manual processes and credible and attractive positioning – is proven. The sum of the parts is shown to be greater than the whole.

Organisations cannot expect those crucial activities to take shape and interlock automatically; the management of people and resources along well-defined paths to meet predetermined strategies will be covered later in the chapter. Marketing can be represented as a pentagram, each of the five Ps forming an arm, with the customers (in their various segments) at the apex. Marketing is the medium through which corporate objectives are turned into bottom-line reality.

SIX PRESSURES TO INNOVATE

The necessity of approaching the market systematically becomes greater daily. Industries which have undergone great change and radical transformations in the last 20 or 30 years have been confronted with pressures to innovate on many fronts – but none with so many as those weighing on the financial services industry at the end of the 1980s.

Profit

The 'cartels' are breaking up; in the last stages of macro global competition, giant companies lost their heads, falling over themselves to lend money abroad, to make acquisitions that cost rather than contributed. The losses that resulted changed the face of British banking forever. The competitive vigour now shown by the leaders in the UK market is not underestimated by peers among banks and competitors such as the building societies. Much of the impetus to change and to enter new markets in the UK has stemmed directly from the setbacks of the last 10 years; the lessons will not be forgotten. Returns to shareholders have become the primary determinant of performance, establishing a standard of success and a measurement method too visible to ignore. Insurance companies, mutuals and societies seek to break out of their cocoons, as owners and investors look for better returns and continuing security in the future.

Competitive advantage

Competitive advantage has not been a phrase well aired in British industry until recently, certainly not in the financial industry. It is still used too frequently in conjunction with the word 'sustainable' when it is clear that such opportunities for a permanent edge rarely exist. Nevertheless competitive intelligence units in marketing departments watch movements in the market like hawks, as do the analysts who watch corporate reactions to market forces, for different reasons. Computer models calculating the benefits of initiating a radical change or the costs of a response to a competitor's lead are constantly updated.

The banks' entry into the mortgage market in the early 1980s is a classic example. It was countered by the building societies' move into banking as the reduced margins on mortgage business forced down their savings rates and encouraged them to look for new profit streams. Today building societies compete on corporate rates for money transmission, offer credit cards and some of the best current account products on the market. The consumer wins and the challenge to improve service, value and performance is constant. The service industry has no short cuts to cost reduction, and the emphasis on product and service value may only be achieved efficiently through precise and effective marketing.

Economic change

All industry is dependent on favourable economic conditions. What constitutes 'favourable' differs from one industry to another. On its current cost base the finance industry suffers as interest rates decline, earning less from the endowment benefit of its mass customer base, too inflexible and unproductive to manage its costs down. Interest rates, exchange rates, inflation rates and the ratios between these will always be changing. National and international economies are being reshaped. Organisations have no option but to change; fundamental restructuring of the balance sheets of such organisations will be accompanied by the need for immeasurably better management information and an understanding of the implications of new product and service development on the balance sheet.

Technological change

No sooner are the rules of the game established and understood than technology introduces new ways of competing. A niche player in the mortgage market can offer competitively priced products and valuable complementary services, such as insurance, to the highest standards of efficiency on a computer-based cost structure that a bank or building society cannot match without using similar technology. Competitive advantage will not so much be taken by the leaders as given up by those who fail to follow fast.

Legislative change

An interesting perspective on the enormous changes that have characterised the financial industries in the last 20 years is that legislation is seen to be the cause of change when in fact it is a symptom. As the plates of market forces move, shift, separate or push together and buckle, so regulators and legislators codify the changes. Financial institutions, largely law-abiding and obedient, are swift and conscientious in their response and absorb the increased costs with little protest. The pattern is likely to remain unchanged until consumers become even more aware of values in financial services and therefore recognise the additional costs of their enforced security. Nevertheless legislative change is a catalyst, and, in gearing up for change, company executives could be using the opportunity to structure their organisations in very untraditional ways to generate competitive advantage. Failure to think laterally will add to cost and complexity and slow the response rate of an organisation.

Social change

Social change will force the most significant innovations on financial organisations. Very few chief executives will have featured 'response to social change' on their list of priorities, nor would it have ranked high in their objectives or job descriptions.

Given a customer relationship that will often last from 16 years to death, and, in the case of corporate relationships, even longer, this is an omission which competition will change. Peter Drucker states it baldly: 'Business has only two basic functions – marketing and innovation.'[1] The latter cannot be achieved at a profit without the former. Marketing which fails to recognise the power of social change will fail. Any organisation ignoring the facts that those parts of the British population who buy financial services are becoming

- older
- wealthier
- better at managing their money
- more aware and more demanding
- very often female

will fall by the wayside.

Each of the three campaigns described in the case histories that follow recognised changes in the market which called for action. The six pressures to innovate and in particular the forces for social change will prevail and accelerate between today and 1999, and will underpin all successful marketing strategies and colour most tactical campaigns.

In the case of CarOwner Plus the action was defensive, the personal loan product on which it was based being a mature one entering the final stages of the product life-cycle, beset on all sides by new, cheaper methods of consumer finance.

In the case of the Credo business start-up loan radical changes in the composition of the British working population and more particularly in the attitudes of the would-be entrepreneurs fell into place when new statistics on the reasons for failure of many new enterprises were published. A very good product, already available at the bank, was reconfigured, repriced and communicated in a fresh way, and had considerable success in attracting the attention of its target group.

The HomeOwner Plus mortgage campaign was different. A strategic decision to double the number of home-owning customers in 1 year and then do the same again over the next 2 years reflected a thorough understanding of major demographic and socio-economic shifts in the population and the importance in volume and value of this customer group for the next 20 years of business. Mortgages have become one of the new core products of the banking business and the basis for a customer relationship which lasts on average for 7 years. They are also an essential element in the bank's image as a provider of consumer finance for the individual. As a profit generator with low risk and high stability, mortgages are second to none, but large volumes of consumer lending have balance-sheet implications for a financial organisation. The 3 years' growth in the mortgage book recognised these implications.

SIGNIFICANT SOCIAL CHANGES

The major social changes referred to in the preamble to the case histories, and which every chief executive or senior partner in a service business should have featured in his or her job description and objectives, are summarised below.

Britain will grow older in the next 10 years

The two fastest-growing groups in the population are aged 25–34 and 45–59. The first group has grown and will grow by 15 per cent, or over 1.3 million people, between 1985 and 1995. (Statistics are provided by the government actuary and the Henley Centre for Forecasting.) The second group has grown and will grow by approximately 10 per cent, or 1 million people, over the same period (Source: Henley Centre for Forecasting). In terms of business potential these two groups are the most profitable.

In Thatcher's home-owning Britain the family formation group is the most active user of all financial services and the 45–59-year-old group has been the beneficiary of wage inflation, which has risen faster than price inflation over the last decade and which looks set to continue. Described by the Henley Centre as 'the empty nesters', this group sees its disposable income increasing at exactly the time that deregulation and competition is causing the creation of interesting and attractive new investment products designed specifically for a more aware and financially sophisticated market. Britain's obsession with marketing to youth is giving way to new preoccupations with young, upwardly mobile, professional people – 'yuppies' for short – and with the 45–59-year-old group.

What of youth? Critically for banks and building societies, the two major age groups in the traditionally targeted youth category are getting smaller. The 15–19-year-old group has fallen and will fall by over 25 per cent between 1985 and 1995 and the 20–24 group by slightly less over the same period. The implications for providers of services for 'new bankers' are clear: supply will exceed demand, the cost of attracting new customers will escalate, and competition will begin with price and develop into new added-value strategies as customers quickly learn to distinguish between price and value. Given that a young person opening a bank account today is still twice as likely to retain that relationship during a lifetime as keep the same spouse, neither banks nor the new entrants to current account banking can sit out of this competition.

Britons will grow wealthier in the next 10 years

The growth pattern of wealth during the last 10 years will be repeated in the next 10 years. In terms of physical assets (homes, property, etc.), Britons' wealth increased by £500bn from 1976 to 1985, from £200bn to

£700bn; in financial assets parallel increases occurred, taking the financial asset base of Britons from £160bn to £600bn (source: OSO Financial Statistics). Add to that growth the benefit of income growth at rates faster than price increases and the value of inheritances over the next decade and the potential of the key age groups is overwhelming.

The first generation of British home-owners and postwar business builders is dying and passing its property and assets on to its middle-aged children. The value of property and possessions inherited in 1987 is estimated at £10bn, with 53 per cent going to the 45–59 age group, 24 per cent to those over 60 and approximately 6.5 per cent to the 25–34-year-olds. By 1997 the gross figure is estimated to reach £24bn, shared in approximately the same proportions, which means that the 45–59s' benefit will be £13.5bn and even those under 45 will enjoy inheritances worth £5.85bn (source: Henley Centre for Forecasting).

Britain is becoming a mass middle-class society

The changes in the national profile of age and wealth focus attention on new marketing directions. Britain is splitting into two nations – the 'haves' and the 'have-nots': specifically the socio-economic groups A, B and C1 have increased by 4.6 per cent since 1971 to a total of 17.8 million people. The increases have been counteracted by a reduction in what was once described as the lower middle class, which has declined by almost exactly the same percentage (4.7 per cent). The socio-economic categories D and E comprise 14.4 million people, but over the last 15 years the 75 : 25 split in favour of D has shifted so that now fully 50 per cent are in the E category.

The marketing and investment implications for financial organisations are clear. Develop new value-added products and services with flexible pricing characteristics for the 'haves' and no-frills products and services for the 'have-nots' or be prepared to give up that business. New technology offers players significant opportunities in both fields, providing they recognise the necessity of dealing with the different categories in different ways and building their strategies on new and lower cost bases.

The rise of 'bourgeois' Britain, as the *Economist* describes it, is matched by significant shifts in attitude on the part of those customers in the upper income and socio-economic categories. Using the word 'assets' in its broadest sense, time, money, knowledge and health are assets. In middle-class Britain in the 1990s the questions will be the following: 'How am I going to accumulate enough knowledge to be able to steer my way through this increasingly complex world but at the same time not be overwhelmed by it?' 'How do I preserve my health, by diet or abstinence from smoking and drinking, so I can be sure of a long life and continued gratification as the return on my investment?' 'Will my savings and my investments allow that deferred gratification in the measure to which I have become accustomed as I move up the income scale?'

In line with the shifts in economic and financial awareness there is a shift in political culture − from state provision to privatisation, from collectivism to individualism, i.e. a rise in the self-help ethic. These characteristics of change are most obvious in the changing distribution of the working population. The implications for the distributors of financial products and services are equally clear.

Changing distribution of the working population

Between 1971 and 1986 the emergence of the new 'post-industrial' society became obvious. Males, representing 52 per cent of the full-time workforce in 1971, had declined to 39.6 per cent by 1986, with unemployment (mainly male) growing from 2.9 per cent to 11.4 per cent. The major growth areas were among females, both full-time (up from 11.3 per cent to 14.8 per cent), part-time (up by 2 per cent to 9.6 per cent) and among the self-employed. Extrapolating from these statistics and drawing trend lines based on more recent evidence, we can see that all providers of financial services will have to amend past practices and assumptions and build new products and establish excellent service standards if they are to satisfy these new customers. The increased proportion of women among first-time home-buyers and entrepreneurs starting new businesses indicates two new types of customer.

A study of projected occupational change by the Warwick Institute for Employment Research shows that the numbers of factory operatives and unskilled labourers will continue to decline, more at the expense of men than women. In contrast, in clerical, sales and secretarial jobs, managerial and supervisory staff and professional roles, which will increase, there will be substantially more female entrants than male. In the period 1984−90 women will outnumber men by 250,000 as new entrants to the professions.

The rise of materialism

In each case of socio-economic change or change in working patterns there has been a change in the signals, too. The status derived from the workplace has diminished and the authority of consumption has risen; to put it another way, people are recognised and evaluated less by how they earn and more by how they spend. It takes little imagination to see how this distinction is given an extra twist by the emergence of the 'connoisseur consumer', where keeping up with the Joneses is less important than being different from them. In all things the attitude of the day now says, 'No, I do not know my place. I am a unique individual and I judge for myself.'

Information growth

As dominant values and authorities decline, as the divergence between the educated and the less educated increases, and sophisticated technology from word processor to the print presses of Wapping bombards us with information, we are overwhelmed. From office in-tray to Sunday newspapers we are assailed by more information than we can read, never mind absorb. Every technique to improve our capacity to assimilate information fails and we look to the information providers to undertake some form of 'editing'. Financial information is among the most complicated confronting people today, protected by the jargon and the mystique of the purveyors. Money must be demystified if it is to be part of the everyday lives of the mass of Britons. Lawyers, accountants, bankers and financial advisers have to bend their efforts to 'editing' information and reducing the confusion gap between continuing information growth and our capacity to assimilate.

Time equals money

There is a value in providing services which are designed to reduce the size of the information gap. Most workers and consumers are aware that at the peak of earnings, time is most limited. At the opposite ends of the spectrum the school pupil, student or pensioner are intensely aware of the fact that time is more available than money. Extraordinary increases in home-delivered food services, micro-wave ready meals, packaged adventure holidays and take-away entertainment show that those with the least time will pay substantial premiums for its preservation. In modern Midland Banking terminology there are money 'managers' and money 'delegators' – the former spend time to save money, the latter spend money to save time. Financial organisations must cater for and profit from both categories.

FREE BANKING – AN EARLY RECOGNITION OF CHANGE

The recognition of the time/money paradox underpinned a fundamental change in the mass marketing of financial services in the UK – a paradigm shift in the economics of the consumer finance industry in this country, which tore a hole in the pricing fabric of personal banking and signalled once and for all that the customer had arrived. The initiative was Free Banking.

Research findings over the two years from 1983 to 1985 made it clear to Midland Bank's marketing department that nearly half its 4.5 million current account base were totally disenchanted by paying bank charges for transactions conducted while in credit. Diminishing returns from existing customers and increasing loss of customers to the smaller banks pointed to an obvious solution. Remove all bank charges for those customers who kept their accounts in credit. The calculation comparing the cost of the income forgone with the benefit of increased market share was more complex. Only if a number of key objectives were achieved would the pre-emptive strike on the other major clearing banks justify the decision in profit terms and stop the attrition in favour of the smaller regional banks. The objectives were clear:

- Specifically target ABC1s; make an unequivocal offer (free if in credit) to the better-off 'money managers'.
- Capture data on those joining Midland so as to achieve maximum sales of additional products and services.
- Achieve a minimum 3-month lead over major clearing bank competitors, so that the volumes of customers transferring in would

be great and rewarding enough to justify the income lost from bank charges forgone by Midland's existing customers in credit.

- Stop the attrition of Midland's market share.

The complex computer models showed that 3 months was the shortest acceptable period of grace; in the event Midland was given 12 months by its competitors, and during that period 750,000 customers left their own banks and opened current accounts with Midland.

- Midland's market share of newly acquired current accounts moved from a 'natural' 16 per cent to over 20 per cent in 1986.
- 65 per cent of them were ABC1, compared with the 56 per cent ABC1 composition of Midland's existing customer base.
- Within the year, often immediately, 30 per cent of them were overdrawing.
- On introducing their own free banking tariff 12 months after Midland, the competitors raised the charges to debit customers by such a significant amount that in matching them Midland's own income and profit was improved by millions of pounds.
- The majority of the 'new' customers, discerning and wealthier, have bought two or more ancillary financial products, in particular mortgages, home equity lines and insurance.

Of all these changes the most significant long-term gain was the upgrading of the customer base towards wealthier and financially more active customers. Using a price-based strategy to improve the customer base conformed precisely to the first step in marketing set out earlier in this chapter – 'Identify the desired customer base'.

THREE CASE HISTORIES

Each of the case histories sets out quite specifically how the five steps in marketing financial services have been approached so far:

1   Identify the desired customer base.

2   Determine the specific needs of the targeted customer group(s).

3   Produce products and services that (a) meet those needs, (b) make profits and (c) differentiate.

4   Communicate and deliver the products or services to the market.

5   Commit the sales force.

CarOwner Plus

CarOwner Plus was an interesting micro-campaign first run in 1986 and repeated with variations since. Its particular characteristics repay study.

The personal loan, a mainstay of the clearing banks' income-generating and customer service activity for many years, was in substantial decline by 1986. The fiercest competition came from the forecourts of car dealers and from car manufacturers working with finance companies to offer the cheapest car-purchase loan schemes. Even the finance house subsidiaries of the main clearers were heavily committed to this market.

At the same time, each year records were being broken for the number of new cars bought and for the number of second-hand cars being released on to the market as larger and larger company fleets turned over a proportion of their cars early each summer in anticipation of the new registrations. Young men in employment continued to trade up over this period and the quality and cost of second-hand car purchases continued to rise.

The banks' share of this business was declining but the personal loan product itself remained extremely profitable. Rather than let this decline continue unabated, Midland determined to reverse this trend by careful identification and analysis of the target market and the development of an improved product to meet the market's needs.

The result was CarOwner Plus, a campaign which lasted for 3 months over the car-buying period in the summer of 1986 and which increased Midland's business on personal loans for cars by 25 per cent, yielding a profit in excess of £1m with little additional workload on the branch network. The ingredients of this campaign seem extraordinarily simple. In the first instance the target market was precisely identified as young men aged 24–30, C1, C2 and D, in employment and in the market for second-hand cars. In addition to the preoccupation with cars, their other interests were easily identified as sport, leisure and music, and their attitudes towards the car purchase were directed as often as not towards the potential influence that such a purchase would have on members of the opposite sex. Careful research identified beyond doubt that the most attractive car in the world for this market was a Porsche 911; on this basis it was decided that the Porsche would become the centrepiece of a major promotion on personal loans. Each successful applicant for a personal loan would have his or her name entered into a raffle drawn sufficiently close to the date of application to make it exciting. It sounds simplistic now but it was a breakthrough in the banks' promotion of personal loans to a specific target market.

The promotional cost, including the purchase of the car, was £435,000. This cost was accurately estimated in advance, as was the cost of administering the personal loan applications in the branches and providing for the increased bad debt that would result from higher volumes of loans. This figure was £209,000, again calculated on a computer model in advance. The net profit for the exercise was £1,149,000.

In addition to this and over the same period, a further 13,000 personal loans were generated for products other than cars; these 13,000 accounts were incremental sales and contradicted the downward trend of personal loan business referred to above. The branch traffic generated was substantial. This was popular with the staff, who were able to cross-sell significant volumes of motor insurance policies, which had been carefully tailored to meet the same marketing requirements.

There are two postscripts to this story. The first is that the winner of the raffle was a female doctor of quite different socio-economic status to the targets, proving that target-marketing is not an exact science. The second postscript is that research among the young males after the promotion indicated that while the Porsche was extremely attractive, the cost implications of insuring it and running it were so substantial as to cause the offer to be changed in subsequent years to something equally racy but more affordable.

Personal loans for cars are once again a field for hot competition between the clearing banks. While margins have been eroded as a result of the increased promotional costs, the business remains profitable, particularly if substantial volume increases are achieved.

HomeOwner Plus

The second case history concerned a fundamental change in the packaging and promotion of mortgages to compete with the clearing banks and some building societies. There were two powerful reasons for undertaking a major onslaught on the mortgage market in 1986. The first of these concerns the demographic changes referred to earlier in this chapter, in particular the ageing of the British population and the increasing numbers of prospective home-buyers entering the market for the first time. The postwar baby boom swelled the family formation and home-owning age group. Conservative government policies of the last 10 years have fuelled the dramatic transformation in home-owning statistics. By 1995 the number of people in the 25–34-year-old age group will have grown by approximately 1.3 million, presenting an opportunity which a financial organisation enjoying a lifetime relationship with a customer cannot afford to ignore.

In addition to the volume increase in the market segment, a second reason for the commitment to the mortgage business by a clearing bank is the average 7-year life of a mortgage before it is renewed. These 7 years coincide with the peak levels of financial activity by the age group. Considerable opportunities for profit and the opportunity to cement the relationship between bank and customer make the mortgage an essential item in the service offer at a time of increasing volatility and rising numbers of account transfers between banks and building societies.

Using the principles established in CarOwner Plus, careful research was undertaken to determine the preoccupations of this much larger and more broadly based group of potential customers; the research findings provided a clear guide to the preoccupations of home-buyers and therefore to the key elements of the promotion:

- *Price*. Research indicates that many existing mortgage customers cannot accurately quote their current mortgage rate. This, however, is not true for those entering into a new mortgage. Price sensitivity is crucial for the new mortgage customer.

- *Associated costs*. There is a widespread perception that the costs associated with a mortgage are very substantial. Once again research indicated that many prospective home-buyers could not quote even a moderately accurate figure.

- *Availability of funds.* There was some fear, even among customers who had been saving for a mortgage with a building society or bank, that they would not have ready access to the funds as soon as they required them or found a home. This fear was belied by the open-handedness of financial organisations at the time of the HomeOwner Plus promotion, but remained an important preoccupation of prospective customers.
- *Transfer costs.* Those customers aware of transferring a mortgage from one institution to another once again perceived these costs to be high.
- *Moving-in costs.* Finally, research clearly indicated what most home-buyers know – the cost of moving into a home is only one small part of starting life there. The necessity of furnishing a home and handling the budgets remained a further cause for anxiety.

The HomeOwner Plus promotion sought to tackle each of these concerns in a precise and straightforward manner. The television and press advertising campaigns were startlingly different and carried a message that precisely responded to the carefully researched needs stated above:

- *Price* – a half per cent off the cost of the mortgage for the first 12 months.
- *Associated costs* – a £50 cashback to help with solicitor's fees was not a substantial offer when compared with the absolute level of charges, but it was an indication that the practicalities of home moving were understood.
- *Availability of funds* – a mortgage certificate provided to young house-purchasers by the bank allowed them to shop with confidence, knowing that they had the funds available for any property within their price range.
- *Transfer costs* – a free transfer from competing institutions made the items listed above still more attractive to those customers aware that these charges existed.
- *Moving-in costs* – interest-free loan repayments for the first year were a further modest recognition by the bank that moving into a new home cost money.

The response to the campaign was overwhelming. By the end of the 12-month period and after a promotion which had only lasted 1 month, business had increased from £1.3bn to £2.75bn. Midland's market share among the four main clearing banks had increased over this period from 12 per cent to 22 per cent. In the process it had gained 56,000 new customers, 80 per cent of whom were ABC1s. This reinforced the shift towards more profitable customer groupings first undertaken in the free banking campaign 2 years before.

Of the new customers, 90 per cent transferred from the competition, and the cross-sales of products in 1986 were substantial and largely concentrated on insurance. Between 1986 and 1988 these cross-sales continued unabated, and now extend across the full range of traditional and new banking products and into the new set of personal financial services permitted by recent legislation. Home-owners are significant buyers of unit trusts, other forms of insurance and, increasingly, of pensions.

The 1987 and 1988 campaigns used fundamentally the same mechanics, because preliminary research showed that the basic package still met customers' needs. Temporary price reduction, discounts on loan rates, straightforward presentation of the benefits to customers in the press and in-branch displays ensured that all profit targets were met, though fluctuating interest rates affected volumes or margins each year.

The difficulty was that the success of the HomeOwner Plus campaigns in 1986 and 1987 had attracted competitors to match the promotional items, point by point, even to simple variations on the name. By 1988 Midland's offer was no longer seen as different. Surplus funds that had flowed into building societies' savings accounts were released into the mortgage market and the offer, basically the same as that of 1986 and 1987, was wrapped into a new communications package bearing the brand name 'Orchard'. Branding and related themes will not be developed here but will form one part of the third case history, set out below.

CREDO Small Business Packages: the Five Essential Steps

In the most recent of the three business initiatives, the case history shows how the five essential steps have been followed precisely to a satisfactory conclusion. CREDO, a new business start-up package, was launched in 1987. The package of advice and banking services had been designed, step by step, to achieve differentiation in the small-business market-place.

1 *Identify the desired customer base*
   This is a highly profitable market, as evidenced by a Midland Strategic Business Unit study, which indicated bottom-line profitability approaching £100m for the Small Business Sector in 1987 and projected profits in excess of that in 1988. Financial projections for CREDO forecast an incremental average year profit of over £2m per annum and a year ending 1989 return on equity well above the historic norms for a banking business. Start-up businesses, a growing phenomenon in the late 1980s and interestingly often started (43 per cent) by women, were the target.

   This was in an environment where many business start-ups failed in a short space of time and there was an unwelcome associated high bad-debt ratio. It was of paramount importance to address the issue, both to help protect the new business customer from a preventable early demise and the bank from unnecessary bad debt. The resulting CREDO package fully recognised the risk dynamics of the small business market.

2 *Determine the specific needs of the targeted customer groups*
   There was already in place a business start-up package comprising all the elements of advice and banking facilities that one would expect from a UK clearing bank. All these elements were analysed, then redesigned and repackaged into a set of guidebooks and advisory leaflets to help the would-be entrepreneur. The package was divided into two parts – Planning and Banking – to fit the two different needs of such individuals.

   Part One – Planning – was targeted specifically at those who have not yet taken the first step into business but are seeking advice and guidance. Enterprise agencies, accounting and law firms and Midland's own Direct Mail unit provided additional delivery outlets.

   Part Two – Banking – was designed to meet the needs not only of those passing through the Planning phase but also to win new accounts outright from the competition. Initial market research revealed that over 90 per cent of the respondents were positive to the whole package.

3 *Produce products and services that (a) meet those needs, (b) make profits, and (c) differentiate*
   From the bank's viewpoint CREDO was specifically designed to meet the following objectives:

Marketing in practice for financial services

- Meet identified needs in the manner described above.

- Increase market share of new small businesses – Midland's share, at 16 per cent, compared unfavourably with NatWest (30 per cent) and Barclays (25 per cent).

- Reduce the risk associated with attracting young businesses, where our bad-debt experience had historically been high.

- Provide a future profitable base of business account customers.

- Increase sales of business current accounts and thereby improve cross-selling.

- Establish the company's image as an intelligent provider of business services.

The two-part CREDO package fulfilled two needs – advice and guidance, and business banking. The first part of the package became overnight the definitive training model for business colleges and enterprise agencies. The second part, CREDO-Banking, which incorporated eight account-opening offers carefully designed to meet identified needs, has resulted in the opening of 43,000 new small business accounts since 1987.

The shelf life of the eight account-opening offers varied, but none was intended to be long-term and the literature was therefore designed to allow additions or deletions at any time. The finance offers were subject to normal lending criteria, which could have included the need for security or an acceptable business plan. The latter was addressed by specialist training packages for customers and staff and improved credit-scoring systems for branches. The opening offers included:

- overdraft – 3 months free up to £1000

- loan – 0.5 per cent discount if insurance taken

- tariff – first two quarters free and fixed thereafter

- accounting – discount on purchase of proprietary manual accounting system

- training – discounted purchase option on Rapid Results correspondence courses

- insurance – free consultation with insurance brokers
- invitation – free discussion and counselling session after 9 months
- Enterprise Allowance Scheme – 12 months' commission-free banking.

From this list it will be evident that the principles of research, analysis, targeting and matching needs and benefits demonstrated in the first two case histories have been assiduously pursued.

As regards differentiation, in terms of a business strategy CREDO was the first stage in a campaign to deliver packaged business products to defined market segments.

It was envisaged that CREDO would be the core proposition and that future small-business propositions would use the CREDO branding. The launch of CREDO in 1987 established the product, the name of a small-business brand and the associated logo. **Where products and prices are at parity the only possible differentiator is the quality of service and the external communications, particularly the use of branding.**

The package was important also because it represented a significant and fundamental change in the company's approach to the small-business sector, and as such the business strategy called for the development of internal procedures in close liaison with Retail Credit and Risk. In particular, an improved mandatory credit scoring system for small-business customers was developed. This was a clear example of the interrelationship between the products, processes and people of the five Ps.

In a risk-averse culture it was also necessary for the company to investigate staff behaviour in Risk/Reward lending and establish improved education and training courses where a need was identified. The risk dynamics, which had been carefully researched within the Small Business Sector, are complex and the company's bad-debt experience is high. In 1986 provisions totalling £15m were raised against approximately 12,000 accounts with annual turnover less than £100,000. Statistics from external sources revealed that 30 per cent of businesses fail within 2 years of start-up. This figure is reduced to 17 per cent if advice is taken (e.g. from an enterprise agency) *but only 10 per cent fail if advice and practical guidance are taken* (e.g. training).

4 *Communicate and deliver to the target segment*
In the end the proposition was simple but powerful. Projects were actually made more difficult for the would-be entrepreneur by the bank's demanding a business plan. Given that such a plan improves the chances of success from 1 in 10 to 1 in 6 and that a top-notch plan improves the success rate still further to 1 in 3, then the business plan hurdle is a good thing for customer and bank alike. As a major incentive the banking offer rewards the careful planner with an unsurpassed range of benefits.

A whole panoply of communications media were used externally, which is normal for a major new launch. This included:

- TV
- Press
- Branch literature (including suppliers of accounting and training services)
- Branch training material
- Training video
- Branch displays at point of sale
- PR launch
- Regional presentations.

The branch network was well and truly ready for the onslaught.

5 *Commit the Sales force*
In addition to the new credit-scoring system and the usual service details which a bank communicates by Head Office circular, there was a set of product knowledge training modules and a specially developed and major Skill Development Programme for branch staff and team leaders. This, together with a carefully focused incentive scheme triggered when key targets were reached, ensured the full and wholehearted commitment of the branch staff – the sales force.

The end results of the campaign have yet to be fully evaluated but all volume targets have been exceeded and projections for the future are strong.

IN SUMMARY

1 *ORGANISATION*

Organise the business so that those responsible for its main strands can work in concert towards the pre-determined ends. Bind Products, Premises, People, Processes and Positioning into a coherent whole and work at the synergies. Marketing is not an activity conducted by one department on behalf of the organisation but a state of mind which permeates every activity within the business.

2 *MARKETING*

Organise the marketing department's effort so that it flows sequentially and systematically from Research and Analysis through Product Development and Management to Communications and Packaging (internal is as important as external).

3 *MARKETS AND ACTIVITIES*
- Fix the target market.
- Establish income and volume expectations.
- Identify the triggers or calls to action of that market.
- Develop the products.
- Communicate – internally and externally.
- Measure results and analyse.
- Start again.

4 *BUDGETS*
- Fix the target market.
- Establish volume and value expectations.
- Develop products. Establish cost of sale and margins.
- Calculate cost of promotional activity.
- Forecast contribution/profit.
- Measure results and analyse.
- Adjust and start again.

5 THE FIVE ESSENTIAL STEPS

- Identify the desired customer base.
- Determine the specific needs of the targeted customer group(s).
- Produce products and services that (a) meet those needs, (b) make profits, and (c) differentiate.
- Communicate and deliver the products or services to the market.
- Commit the sales force.

REFERENCE

1 Drucker, Peter *Management: Tasks, Responsibilities, Practices* (Heinemann, 1974)

INDEX

accountants, 171–2, 186, 191, 192, 198, 202, 212, 220
- assessing markets, 177–80
- consideration of markets, 173–5
- outside assistance, 184–5
- planned approach to marketing, 172–3
- promotional activities, 172, 175, 180, 181, 182, 184
- skill development, 181, 185
- target markets, 175–7, 180, 183
- see also advertising; budgets; competition; customer requirements; marketing; media, the; presentation and selling policy; promotion; public relations

Acorn, 124
Advertisers' Annual, 132, 138, 139, 140, 144
advertising, 1–2, 14, 18, 29, 32, 33, 34, 35, 37, 41, 99, 112, 113, 114, 116, 119, 120–25, 130, 141, 142, 149, 152, 168, 178, 181, 183, 199
- agencies, 128, 129, 130, 131–4, 135, 136, 137, 139, 142, 143, 160
- see also Incorporated Society of British Advertisers (ISBA); Institute of Practitioners in Advertising; market research; promotional literature; writing

Advertising Association, 28, 42, 143
Allen, Norman, 119
Allen, Woody, 204
Ashridge Management College, 42, 97

Barclays, 221
Bateson, J.E.G., 18, 19, 20, 21, 23, 164
Bradford University, 25, 40, 41
Brewer, Michael, 101
British Direct Marketing Association, 139, 143
British Institute of Management, 42
British Media Publications, 144
British Rate and Data (BRAD), 139, 140, 144
Brown, Ian, 65
budgets, 11, 34, 35, 37, 115–17, 120, 121, 124, 134, 141, 142, 143, 181, 183, 218, 224
- see also financial services; planning and budgeting; price; pricing strategy; promotion

[227]

business plan, 102, 221, 222, 223, 224
  detailed forecasts, 100
  detailed planning, 94–5
  environment, 88–90, 96–7
  finance, 99
  mission statement, 91–2, 93, 96
  operational planning, 93–4
  planning as management technique, 85–6, 89
  planning cycle, 87–8
  planning process, 86–7, 90
  premises and equipment, 98
  review and control, 95, 100
  staffing, 98
  see also competition; corporate identity; CREDO; Executive Educators Ltd (EEL); financial services; marketing; planning and budgeting; professional advisers; strategic marketing planning

CAM Foundation, 28–9, 31, 42
Carlzon, Jan, 70, 71
CarOwner Plus, 208, 215–16, 217
  see also Porsche
Chartered Institute of Marketing, 2, 5, 10, 17, 25, 28, 31, 42, 65, 139, 144
College of Marketing, 25, 32, 42, 65
communications, 153, 156, 157, 164, 184, 198, 201, 202, 203, 208, 215, 219, 222, 223, 224, 225
  available options, 122–4
  cost-effectiveness, 125
  creative element, 124–5
  first principles, 119–20
  see also advertising; marketing communications; media, the; presentation and selling policy; public relations; speaking; writing

company strategy, 18–19, 221
  see also business plan; consumer behaviour; corporate identity; Executive Educators Ltd; financial services; Product Portfolio Analysis; professional advisers; strategic marketing planning

competition, 8, 9, 10, 11, 13, 14–15, 23, 34, 46, 47, 49, 50, 55, 64, 74, 75, 79, 82, 89, 97, 99, 102, 107, 108, 110, 141, 149, 155, 156, 157, 164, 174, 175, 176, 177, 186, 191–2, 194, 204, 205–6, 207, 209, 213, 214, 215, 216, 217, 218, 219, 220

computer market, 160
'connoisseur consumer', 212
  see also consumer behaviour
Constable, J., 96
consulting engineers, 159, 160–65, 169
consumer behaviour, 33, 38, 41, 213
  see also 'connoisseur consumer'
corporate identity, 2, 90–91, 105, 141
  see also company strategy
Cranfield School of Management, 42, 97
CREDO, 208, 219–22
customer care, 70–72
  see also intercustomer influence
customer requirements, 23, 36
  anticipating them, 10, 17, 156, 157, 158, 169, 186, 188, 189, 191, 196, 215, 220, 225

[228]

identifying them, 10, 13, 15, 17, 48, 50, 120, 140, 173–4, 175, 176, 179–80, 181, 188, 189, 191, 193, 203, 213–14, 215, 220, 221, 224, 225
  meeting, satisfying them, 2, 9, 10, 12, 13, 17, 45, 48–9, 56, 117, 164, 166, 174, 186, 188, 189, 191, 194, 196, 197, 203, 215, 219, 220, 221, 225
  see also marketing strategy; professional advisers
customer segmentation, 15–16, 223
  see also marketing: targets
customer viewpoint, 109–10

data collection
  analysis, 59
  data bases, 55
  field research, 56
  interviewing, 58
  published information, 53–5
  questionnaires, 56–7
  reporting, 59
  respondents, 56
  sampling, 57–8
  services, 62–3
  see also market research
Dearsly, Nigel, 159
decision-making unit (DMU), 82, 161
Design Centre, 138
designers and art studios, 129, 138
Dialog, 55
'Differential Advantage', 14–15
  see also unique selling proposition
direct mail, 33, 34, 35, 112, 116, 120, 125, 133, 152, 181, 220
Direct Mail Producers Association, 144
Direct Mail Sales Bureau, 144
direct response marketing, 35

distribution, 2, 9, 11, 27, 37, 66, 112, 195, 203, 204, 211
Doyle, Professor, 14
Drucker, Peter, 10, 12, 101, 207

Economist, The, 210
Enterprise Allowance Scheme, 222
  see also financial services
Essex Business, 123
Executive Educators Ltd (EEL), 96, 97–8, 99
exhibitions, 112, 116, 129, 133, 136, 139, 143, 152, 181

fast-moving consumer goods (FMCG), 34, 201
financial services
  economic change, 206, 211
  free banking, 213–14, 222
  legislative change, 207, 219
  marketing, 201–4, 224
  Skill Development Programme, 223
  social change, 207–13
  technological change, 206
  see also budgets; CarOwner Plus; competition; CREDO; customer requirements; Enterprise Allowance Scheme; HomeOwner Plus; marketing; marketing education; marketing training; OSO Financial Statistics; place; planning and budgeting; positioning; presentation and selling policy; price; process; product; profit; promotion; sales force

Gavaghan, Kevin, 201
Gumbrell, Leslie, 5
Gummerson, Evert, 20

Hall, Robert, 187
Handy, C., 71, 96
Hart, Norman, xi, 25
Harvard University, 32
Henley Centre for Forecasting, 209, 210
Henley Management College, 42
Hertzberg, F.H., 75
HomeOwner Plus, 208, 217–19
hospital market, 160
Humphrey, G.V., xi

'Image Audit', 81
IMEDE, 97
Incorporated Society of British Advertisers (ISBA), 42, 132, 138, 144
industrial marketing, 34, 41
    techniques, 159–65
'industry averages', 142
Infoline, 55
INSEAD, 32, 97
Institute of Export, 31
Institute of Practitioners in Advertising, 28, 132, 144
Institute of Public Relations, 28, 39, 42, 135, 144
Institute of Sales Promotion, 139, 144
intellectual property, 65–6, 69, 71, 74, 75, 76, 80
Interact International Limited, 42
intercustomer influence, 76–8, 82

Kent Life, 123
Kompass, 162
Kotler, Philip, 11–12

Law Society, 199
Levitt, Theodore, 13, 19, 47
Lindsay, Keith, 171
London Business School, 32, 42, 97

London Chamber of Commerce, 27

mailing houses, 129, 138–9
management and business consultants, 160, 172
Management Charter Initiative, 96, 99
Manchester Business School, 97
market research, 33, 34–5, 37, 40, 41, 46, 47, 48, 49, 51–3, 55, 56, 60, 63, 64, 74, 82, 83, 129, 132, 157, 161, 168, 220
    see also data collection; professional markets
Market Research Society, 31, 42, 139, 144
marketing
    assessment, 45–7, 87–8, 96–7, 145–58, 165, 177–80, 187, 192, 198
    creating and developing, organising, 3, 6–8, 127–8, 191
    definition, 1–2, 5–12, 13, 17, 160, 188
    external support services, 140–43
    targets, 98–9, 140, 174, 175–7, 180, 183, 190, 193, 194, 195, 202, 203, 207, 208, 213–15, 216, 220, 222, 223, 224, 225
    see also accountants; advertising; customer requirements; direct response marketing; exhibitions; financial services; industrial marketing; Marketing Society; media, the; place; printers; process; product; public relations; sales prospecting; service marketing; strategic marketing; strategic marketing planning; telemarketing
marketing associations, 39, 42

[230]

Index

see also British Direct
 Marketing Association
marketing communications, 28, 41,
 131, 132
 see also communications
marketing education
 academic marketing education,
  29–30
 marketing qualifications, 27, 39
 need for, 25–7, 222
 professional marketing education,
  27–9
 see also marketing training
Marketing Improvements Limited,
 42
marketing management, 28, 41
 see also consumer behaviour;
  planning and budgeting; price;
  product: development; sales
  management
marketing mix see place; price;
 process; product; promotion;
 positioning
marketing programmes, 46, 51, 53,
 127, 128, 131, 140, 142, 154,
 197
marketing publications, 43
 see also promotional literature
Marketing Society, 42, 139, 144
marketing strategy, 47–9, 63, 64,
 102, 104, 177, 180, 184, 187,
 195, 208, 222
 see also strategic marketing;
  strategic marketing planning
marketing training
 external courses, 32–3, 221
 in-company training, 30–32
 marketing subject areas, 33–40
 recruiting new staff, 39–40
 staff behaviour and need for
  training courses, 222
 training videos, 223

see also financial services;
 marketing associations;
 marketing education;
 marketing publications
McCormick, R., 96
McIver, Colin, 159
media, the, 121–3, 129–30, 134,
 139–40, 143, 152, 153, 154,
 168, 178, 180, 181, 183–4, 185,
 195, 218, 219, 223
 see also British Media
  Publications; *British Rate and
  Data (BRAD)*; *PIMS*
Midland Banking, 213–15, 219, 221
Midland Strategic Business Unit,
 220
Moriarty, R.T., 18
Morse, Stephen, 13, 159

NatWest, 221
Nexis, 55

'one-stop shop', 132
'Orchard', 219
OSO Financial Statistics, 210
ownership, 66, 75

perishability of services, 66,
 72–4
Peters and Waterman, 91
Pilkingtons, 75
PIMS, 140, 144
place, 7, 8, 10, 11, 66, 103, 112,
 204, 219, 224
planning and budgeting, 33, 37
 see also business plan
Porsche, 216
 see also CarOwner Plus
positioning, 204, 224
presentation and selling policy, 2, 9,
 16, 67, 114, 156, 164–5, 181,
 182, 185, 188, 193, 194, 219,
 223

[231]

see also promotion
price, 7, 8, 9, 10, 11, 33, 37–8, 66, 74, 103, 105, 109, 110, 112, 148, 150, 208, 209, 217, 218, 222
pricing strategy, 2, 9, 73, 210, 214
printers, 129, 130, 138, 142
process, 78–80, 204, 224
product, 7, 8, 10–11, 35, 66, 76, 78, 103, 105, 106, 109, 110, 112, 113, 114, 117, 140, 148, 150, 153, 162, 163, 188, 189, 194, 195, 196, 197, 198, 202, 203, 204, 208, 215, 219, 222, 224
    definition, 16, 106–8, 111
    development, 33, 37, 201, 202, 224
    differentiation, 8–9, 187, 203, 215, 219, 220, 222, 225
    value-added, 209, 210
Product Portfolio Analysis, 18
professional advisers, 86, 89, 156, 160, 164, 166, 178
    developing a strategic matrix, 21–2, 23
    executive multiplier, 80–81
    expertise, 19–21, 23
    identifying benefits to clients, 16–17
    information gathering, 81–3
    managing portfolio of clients, 22–3
    nature of professional service business, 66–70, 80
    need to make profit, 17
    reassessing the market, 13–14
    see also company strategy; customer care; customer segmentation; marketing; ownership; perishability of services; product; definition; profit; service marketing; service triangle
professional markets, 59–60

intangibility of the offer, 61
local markets, 61
organisational form, 61
professional's relationship with clients, 60–61
purchasing, 60
sensitivity of services, 60
see also marketing education
profit, 33, 37–8, 74, 148, 149, 150, 174, 191, 193, 194, 203, 204, 205, 206, 215, 216, 217, 219, 220, 221, 224, 225
    see also budgets; business plan; financial services; price; pricing strategy; professional advisers
promotion, 1, 7–8, 9, 10, 11, 34, 66, 75, 76, 103, 112, 113, 114–16, 148, 149, 150, 157, 158, 172, 175, 180, 181, 182, 184, 188, 190, 199, 203, 216, 217, 218, 219, 224
    see also accountants; budgets; presentation and selling policy; sales promotion
promotional literature, 2, 34, 112, 114, 120, 132, 143, 168, 181, 182, 220, 221, 223
    see also advertising; market research; marketing publications; sales promotion
public relations, 2, 18, 29, 33, 34, 35, 41, 112, 114, 119–20, 123, 124, 128, 133, 135–7, 140, 142, 153, 158, 160, 185, 223
see also Institute of Public Relations
Public Relations Consultants Association, 135, 144

Randall, Geoffrey, 85
Rapid Results correspondence course, 221

Index

Retail Credit and Risk, 222
retail locations, 116
Richmond Group, 160
Rotary, 132
Royal Society of Arts, 27

Saatchi brothers, 90
Salamander Estates Limited, 159, 165–9
sales force, 215, 223, 225
   see also financial services; Skill Development Programme
sales management, 27, 33, 38, 168
sales planning, 106, 108–11
sales promotion, 29, 33, 34, 37, 132, 139
   see also Institute of Sales Promotion
sales prospecting, 51–2
Scandinavian Airlines System, 70
selling, 33, 36, 37
   see also presentation and selling policy
service marketing, 70, 75
   see also customer care; ownership; perishability of services; professional advisers
service triangle, 78–80
Shell, 89
Skinner, Richard N., 145
Small Business sector, 222
   see also CREDO
solicitors, 18, 178, 187–9, 202, 212, 218, 220
   constraints, 199
   involving management team, 193–4
   need to market, 198
   need to plan, 190–91
   provision of resources, 195–6
   review machinery, 196–7
   see also competition; customer requirements; Law Society; marketing; presentation and selling policy; product; speaking; writing
Sony Walkman, 105–6
speaking, 33, 36, 125, 194, 196
spreadsheets, 100
strategic marketing, 33, 37, 40
strategic marketing consultants, 184
strategic marketing planning, 94, 101–2, 196
   objectives, 104–6, 114
   planning, 102–3, 111–13
   preparation, 102
   structure, 103
   see also budgets; business plan; competition; customer viewpoint; distribution; marketing strategy; place; presentation and selling policy; price; product; promotion; sales planning
strategy *see* company strategy; marketing strategy; pricing strategy
Strathclyde University, 30
SWOT, 90, 91, 94

telemarketing, 33, 35–6
Textline, 55
Thatcher, Margaret, 209
Thomson, 180

unique selling proposition, 14
   see also 'Differential Advantage'
USM, 96

Warwick Institute for Employment Research, 211
West, Christopher, 45
writing, 33, 36, 103, 128, 132, 136, 140, 181, 182, 184, 194, 195, 196